Young women and girls toda[...]
expectations that are unheal[...]
this book make a valuable co[...]
we can help young women t[...]
freedom and strength to be th[...]

MW00985897

—THE HON. KATE ELLIS, MINISTER FOR EARLY CHILDHOOD EDUCATION, CHILDCARE AND YOUTH, PARLIAMENT OF AUSTRALIA

Congratulations to Melinda Tankard Reist and the writers of *Getting Real* for 'Getting it Right,' for calling it like it is, exposing medicalisation, commercial sexualisation and objectification of our girls, drawing the parallels with sexual assault, anorexia, bulimia and suicide.

Every girl deserves a childhood full of love, trust and support to grow in safety and happiness. Not to be seen as 'thin, hot, sexy' but as 'unique, adorable, talented.' It is time to speak up for the right of every child to grow freely with hope.

Each one of us who cares about a daughter, sister, niece or friend needs to take personal responsibility and join this call demanding a future free of exploitation for all our girls. Parents, teachers, girls themselves and all those who care about and work with girls should read this book.

—COLEEN CLARE, CEO, CENTRE FOR EXCELLENCE IN CHILD AND FAMILY WELFARE

Our modern culture is preoccupied with sexualising the experiences of childhood. *Getting Real* unmasks the tactics of those who mercilessly target children with messages that confuse and distort their development. It offers insights about how to reclaim childhood and support the critical discourse of children's rights.

—JOE TUCCI, CEO, AUSTRALIAN CHILDHOOD FOUNDATION

This book does a wonderful job of adding a much needed feminist approach to the debate on the sexualization of girls. By exploring the issue from a number of perspectives, *Getting Real* brings into stark focus the social and psychological costs of turning our girls into sex objects—costs that we ignore at our peril.

—GAIL DINES PhD, PROFESSOR OF SOCIOLOGY AND WOMEN'S STUDIES AT WHEELOCK COLLEGE AND AUTHOR OF *PORNLAND: HOW PORN HAS HIJACKED OUR SEXUALITY*

Getting Real is an important contribution to the discussion of the sexualisation of girls. This profoundly disturbing issue is a public health problem of international concern. This book is essential reading for parents, educators, and everyone who wishes to make the world a safer and healthier place for all children.

—JEAN KILBOURNE, EdD, AUTHOR OF *SO SEXY SO SOON: THE NEW SEXUALIZED CHILDHOOD AND WHAT PARENTS CAN DO TO PROTECT THEIR KIDS*

If you weren't convinced of the urgency of the situation—this book will light a fire in your efforts to change the world for the next generation. Everyone should read it!

—CAPTAIN DANIELLE STRICKLAND, SOCIAL JUSTICE DIRECTOR, SALVATION ARMY

Getting Real unflinchingly tracks the abuse that, with the pervasive penetration of pornography, becomes normal culture. In the sexuality where objectification of children and infantilization of women converge, the less power you have, the sexier you are. Girls increasingly live in a world pornography has made. This book shows what needs to be stopped and why.

—CATHARINE A. MACKINNON, ELIZABETH A. LONG PROFESSOR OF LAW, UNIVERSITY OF MICHIGAN LAW SCHOOL, AND JAMES BARR AMES VISITING PROFESSOR OF LAW, HARVARD LAW SCHOOL

This is an outstanding collection of contributions addressing a significant problem in our community, namely the abuse of children and particularly girls by sexualising and exploiting them for commercial gain. Most people would be justifiably critical of child prostitution as many of the authors are, but few realise that some of the most respected commercial organisations in our community have no compunction in effectively doing so by their similar abuse of children in advertising. This book fills a real gap.

—THE HON ALASTAIR NICHOLSON AO, FORMER CHIEF JUSTICE OF THE FAMILY COURT AND FOUNDING PATRON OF CHILDREN'S RIGHTS INTERNATIONAL

Children today are exposed to sexual imagery from their earliest years, to sex as a product and our bodies as commodities. The consequences, particularly for girls, are unmistakably negative.

Getting Real gives the mindlessness of this cultural misdirection a good shake. It does it in straightforward language and with academic attention to detail. This book will be a valuable guide, helping young people reclaim their freedom.

—TIM COSTELLO, CEO, WORLD VISION AUSTRALIA

Getting Real wipes away the hot, sexy sheen of the environment in which girls develop, to reveal the ugliness underneath.

—DR CORDELIA FINE, HONORARY FELLOW, SCHOOL OF PHILOSOPHY, ANTHROPOLOGY AND SOCIAL INQUIRY, UNIVERSITY OF MELBOURNE

Getting Real is powerful, disturbing, confronting. We often hear that young women today have never had it better, but the sexualised world they have to grow up in has nothing to do with empowerment. If we don't challenge what we're beginning to accept as the social norm, the risk to our girls will only continue to grow.

—MELINA MARCHETTA, AUTHOR OF *LOOKING FOR ALIBRANDI*

Photograph: David Reist

Melinda Tankard Reist is a writer, speaker, blogger, media commentator and activist against violence against women, objectification of women and sexualisation of girls. Melinda is author/editor of four books including three Spinifex titles *Defiant Birth: Women who resist medical eugenics* (2006), *Getting Real: Challenging the sexualisation of girls* (2009, in its fourth printing) and *Big Porn Inc: Exposing the harms of the global pornography industry* (2011, co-edited with Abigail Bray). Melinda's opinion pieces appear frequently in Australian media and she is a regular on morning television and current affairs programs. Melinda is named in the Australian Who's Who of Women and the World's Who's Who of Women.

Also by Melinda Tankard Reist

Giving Sorrow Words: Women's Stories of Grief After Abortion

Defiant Birth: Women Who Resist Medical Eugenics

Getting Real

Challenging the Sexualisation of Girls

Edited by Melinda Tankard Reist

SPINIFEX

First published in Australia in 2009 by Spinifex Press
Reprinted 2009, 2010, 2011 (twice), 2012.

Spinifex Press Pty Ltd
504 Queensberry St
North Melbourne, Victoria 3051
Australia
women@spinifexpress.com.au
www.spinifexpress.com.au

© on collection Melinda Tankard Reist, 2009
© on individual contributions remains with the authors, 2009
© on design and typesetting, Spinifex Press, 2009
© on cover image Hailey Bartholomew, 2009

All rights reserved. Without limiting the rights under copyright reserved above, no part of this publication may be reproduced, stored in or introduced into a retrieval system, or transmitted, in any form or by any means (electronic, mechanical, photocopying, recording or otherwise) without prior written permission of both the copyright owner and the above publisher of the book.

Copying for educational purposes:
Information in this book may be reproduced in whole or part for study or training purposes, subject to acknowledgement of the source, and providing no commercial usage or sale of material occurs. Where copies of part or whole of the book are made under part VB of the Copyright Act, the law requires that prescribed procedures be followed. For information contact the Copyright Agency Limited.

Cover image by Hailey Bartholomew: www.youcantbeserious.com.au
Cover design by Deb Snibson, MAPG
Typeset by Emma Statham in 12 pt/14.4 pt Bembo typeface
Printed in Australia by McPherson's Printing Group

National Library of Australia Cataloguing-in-Publication:
    Getting real : challenging the sexualisation of girls /
    edited by Melinda Tankard Reist.

    9781876756758 (pbk.)

    Includes index.
    Bibliography.

    Girls in popular culture.
    Children in advertising.
    Sex in advertising.
    Advertising—Psychological aspects.
    Body image—Social aspects.

    Tankard Reist, Melinda.

    306.40820994

PEFC

PEFC/21-31-16

CONTENTS

ACKNOWLEDGEMENTS

Richest thanks to the contributors who gave so generously of their time, talent and passion to see this book come to fruition: Noni, Emma, Maggie, Lauren, Louise, Clive, Selena, Abigail, Melissa, Renate, Betty, Steve, Tania and Julie. It really has been a pleasure and privilege to work with you all.

To Renate—so good to do another book together. Profound thanks for your commitment to this project, and the enormous support and effort you have given to see it to completion.

Susan, Nikki and Maralann at Spinifex—thanks for all your work too. And to Suzie for copy editing.

Hailey—thanks for the perfect photo and Deb, for turning it into the beautiful cover.

To all the endorsees—thank you for adding your good name to this book.

To all who read and commented on my introduction, sincere gratitude. Helen, your skill with words is impeccable. Michael, your positive response meant a lot to me. Thanks due also to Emma, Anna, Caroline, Betty, Angela and Greg.

I am indebted to Sophie, Nanâ, Andrew and Peter. Your generosity in friendship, wisdom and guidance is so valued. For special personal support also, I thank Anna, Suzy, Catherine, Renate, Helen, Angela, Melinda, Erica, Danni, Maria, Sally-Anne, Shawn, Branka, P & Q, Cliff, Mela and David. Julie, the laughter we share has become as necessary to me as food.

To David (for everything), Ariel, Jordan, Kelsey and Layla.

To Maria and Anna.

To all the girls everywhere (and boys too).

And to all those who want to be part of a new movement for change.

The Right of Children to Be Children

Noni Hazlehurst

During the Second World War, many women left the home for the first time to engage in paid work. This was primarily necessary because so many men were away fighting and somebody had to keep the wheels of industry turning. And there was the added advantage that women worked for less remuneration than men. At war's end, however, it became clear that women would need to step aside and be encouraged to go back home, so that men could take their 'rightful place' as the breadwinners. Understandably, some women weren't all that keen to go back to the way things were. So a massive campaign was mounted to make being a little homemaker seem like an attractive and normal thing for women to aspire to. Glittering new domestic appliances were dressed up as objects of desire in print, radio and television ads, television shows and films featuring 'normal' apple pie families were produced, and 'homemaking' was officially sanctioned as the proper occupation for women in the western world.

Predictably, the next generation jacked up, and the sixties brought about revolutions of all kinds. As a child of the fifties, I spent hours drawing home-plans and bridal gowns, only to reject all that for the far more attractive options that feminism offered when I hit my teens and early twenties. We honestly believed that we could give 50 per cent of the world's population the equality, independence and freedom that had been denied for too long.

I loved the fact that women were encouraged to be strong and independent individuals. We didn't have to wear high heels and make-up if we didn't want to, didn't have to pretend to be girlie if we didn't feel that way, could tell a man to get lost if he made remarks we found demeaning and offensive. I also harboured a desire for the words 'women' and 'hysteria' to never again be mentioned together, and for women to be seen as something other than 'little.' I wanted to have the way females perceive things to be valued, not seen as just 'emotional,' and therefore less important than a strictly 'rational' response. After all, rationality didn't seem to be making the world a better place. And for the life of me, I couldn't understand how anyone could think that playing a role in the world of business was more important or deserving of respect than the role played by women who were rearing children. Like many young women and men in the seventies, I rejected media manipulation and rampant consumerism, and determined that my reality would be a construct chosen by me, not imposed by society's expectations and marketing ploys.

How naive I was, thinking that equality was just around the corner. In this first decade of the new century, I think equality is further away than it's ever been. In fact the forces that we rebelled against have gained strength, and are more pernicious than ever.

It saddens me that many young women who call themselves feminists, and who hold positions of public influence, are acting as apologists for the very agents of inequity that have fuelled my anger for so long. They argue that there's no need to worry, everything's acceptable and anyone who has concerns about the way things are going is just an old-fashioned wowser. There are some academics who claim that young children are media savvy and therefore cannot possibly be exploited. One even said in an interview 'I don't really buy the idea that any group is voiceless or powerless.' They quote relentlessly from one or two studies that support their tenuous position and choose to ignore the growing number of findings contradicting their views, not to mention the swelling numbers of concerned parents, doctors and teachers.

These academics refuse to see the forest for the trees. They argue that things have never been better because we have unprecedented power and choice thanks to new paradigms and technologies. Talk about ivory towers. Talk about fiddling while Rome burns.

We have to wake up and smell the crap. It's everywhere. And the weight of evidence that we are causing irreparable damage to our children is becoming overwhelming. Our children are bombarded on a daily basis with images and concepts that they are not able to assimilate, understand or contextualise, even if they have parents or carers who might try to 'explain.'

New technology puts the world at our disposal, sure, but the version or view of the world that our kids are accessing and having thrust upon them is incredibly limited and negative. They can't access or search for something if they don't know it exists. They have no way of knowing the difference between accurate or inaccurate information, no way of discerning what is trustworthy or unreliable. If women are constantly and overwhelmingly portrayed as sex objects, helpless, simpering idiots, or dried-up old prunes, then that must be the way things are. The media focus on celebrity, sex, diet, wealth and plastic surgery, and the implication that these are the only things that count, is causing our kids' imaginations to atrophy. Ask any school teacher whether kids have changed in the last ten years.

The insistent and ubiquitous presentation of this unbalanced view of the world is nothing less than a form of child abuse. Why is it we kick up such a fuss about junk food and obesity, but are unwilling or unable to tackle the lack of quality sustenance for children's minds and spirits? Just as our bodies bear witness to the food we eat, our cultural conserve is the sum of our experiences and knowledge, and more connections are made in the brain in the first three years than at any other time of life. Suggesting we have a dedicated children's television channel is fine, but how many pre-schoolers control the remote? And putting a television in every room is hardly a solution.

Clearly our children are suffering a cultural drought—and when you're parched, when you're desperate for a drink and you have no other options, you take whatever you can get. But if what you get isn't good enough, it follows that you will be seriously compromised.

In my view, our children's imaginations are dying. Their sense of themselves as worthy, strong individuals who are valued because they are unique is constantly being undermined. Only a few can withstand that sort of pressure. And very few will be in a position to be encouraged to be different, as many of today's young parents don't remember when there were alternative ways of looking at the world and other ways to value an individual's noteworthiness.

I've been accused of 'hysterical hyperbole' by the post-modern fervent intellectual champions of the powerful. That's fine. But I'll keep raising the issue and encouraging the thousands of worried parents, and others who care deeply, to think, to speak up and to demand that children be protected from this subversive and manipulative exploitation.

Noni Hazlehurst, Melbourne, June 2009

INTRODUCTION

The Pornification of Girlhood: We Haven't Come a Long Way Baby

Melinda Tankard Reist

Publicly sexual

In 2009, former Hi-5 children's entertainer Kellie Crawford posed for a lingerie photo shoot for men's magazine *Ralph*. The *Ralph* cover for April features Kellie in tiny knickers and black bra, and shouts 'It's Hi5 Hottie Kellie!' with the subtitle 'Busting out some bedtime stories.' It includes another smaller picture of Kellie in her Hi-5 costume.

In the accompanying interview, Kellie explained that as a children's star, she 'just forgot I was a woman.' She did the photo shoot to 'find the woman in me.'

I responded in media interviews by asking why it was that the Wiggles were not expected to prove their manhood by stripping down to their jocks and having their photos taken for a magazine shoot, yet women were expected to take off most of their clothes to prove their womanhood? Opponents of my position, both men and women, filled my inbox with intellectually challenging arguments. These included:

That I was sad, old and dog-ugly

That I had saggy breasts and a droopy arse

That I needed liposuction

That I was a bitter ugly woman

That my face would break a 60-inch plasma television

And, my personal favourite, that I was 'as ugly as a hat full of arses' (obviously not a hat full of Kellie's arses, because hers was magnificent, according to her fans) (email correspondence, April 2009).

However, one little girl in Victoria who seemed not to care about whether I was bitter or needed cosmetic surgery, wrote (email April 20, 2009, used with permission):

> My name is Delaney and I am 10 years old. On Today Tonight I saw a story about Kellie from Hi-5. Of course, you know that she has done a photo shoot for a men's magazine. I think it is very silly how she feels she has to do it. It sets a horrible example for younger kids like me. When I was little I used to love watching Hi-5 and it makes me feel dissappointed [sic] that she has done something like that.

Delaney, and girls like her, receive messages from every level of the media and popular culture that the baring of the female body is what makes you a 'real woman.' Very few young girls have Delaney's courage to distance themselves from this message. Ideal womanhood is now all about sexual allure; the ability to attract the male gaze has become what is important in life. As Pamela Paul writes in *Pornified*, 'being publicly sexual has become the only acceptable way for girls to demonstrate maturity' (2005, p. xxiv).

Putting yourself on show for the sexual gratification of others is what counts. Look at what happened after Susan Boyle's stunning performance of 'I have a dream' on *Britain's Got Talent* which had attracted 100 million YouTube hits at time of writing (June 2009). One of her first offers was from a porn film company keen to 'relieve her of her virginity'—on film of course (http://evilbeetgossip.film.com/2009/04/22/susan-boyle-offered-1m-to-lose-her-virginity-on-camera/).[1]

The sexualisation industry has a voracious appetite for appropriating and corrupting people and things deemed 'innocent,' and remaking them in their own image. There are thousand of porn sites featuring children's cartoon characters. And a growing number of sites depicting the 'defloration' of young girls.

Bearing the brunt

Getting Real: Challenging the Sexualisation of Girls argues that girls should not be objectified in this way. Girls are worth so much more than this. Our contributors take us on a troubling journey across the culture in which we are trying to raise happy, healthy, resilient girls, and demonstrate that much needs to change if this is ever going to be possible. Collectively and compellingly, the writers here show how adult sexual concepts are seeping into girlworld, co-opting girls into a XXX world well before they understand what is happening.

Even in ordinary everyday places, there is material that is deeply disturbing. Julie Gale, for example, exposes porn magazines sold in corner stores, milkbars and petrol stations, as well as porn-related products found in family shopping malls. Some readers might take offence at what appears in this book and wish they hadn't picked it up. But care needs to be taken not to shoot the messenger. We should be troubled and disturbed by the way pornified messaging stalks girls and boys and threatens their healthy development.

---

1 Not that Susan hasn't been humiliated before. Twenty years earlier, when she appeared on another talent show, *My Kind of People*, judge Michael Barrymore spent half the performance lying on the floor looking up her dress. After standing up, he ran his hands around his crotch area, while she continued to sing 'I don't know how to love him' from Jesus Christ Superstar. At the end he grabbed Susan and forced his lips onto her mouth (it would be a misuse of the word to call it a kiss): http://www.youtube.com/watch?v=0g9WS3z3jAw

Girls are facing unprecedented social pressure, their emotional and psychological well-being at risk in many new ways. In *The Body Project: An Intimate History of American Girls*, Joan Jacobs Brumberg writes: 'More than any other group in the population, girls and their bodies have borne the brunt of twentieth-century social change, and we ignore that fact at our peril' (1997, p. 214). The proliferation and globalisation of sexual imagery, along with sexualised clothing, music, games and magazine content for girls, and the social imperative of a perfect body, are all part of this social change.

The pressure to conform to an idealised body type in a sex-saturated culture that values girls who are thin, hot, sexy and 'bad' is taking a terrible toll. Despite the many opportunities at school, university and in the workplace available to them, girls today are struggling. Courtney E. Martin (2007) describes it as 'the frightening new normalcy of hating your body.' Self-hatred is so prevalent, it's like a rite of passage for teenage girls.

The 2007 report of the American Psychological Association (APA) Task Force on the Sexualisation of Girls (APA TSG, 2007, p. 3) links the objectifying and sexualising of girls and young women with the most common health problems suffered by them.

Objectification is reinforced through embedded sexual content everywhere we look. According to the APA, 'A culture can be infused with sexualised representations of girls and women, suggesting that such sexualisation is good and normal' (p. 3). The Report argues that this leads to girls and women feeling bad about themselves (p. 23):

> ...there is evidence that sexualisation contributes to impaired cognitive performance in college-aged women, and related research suggests that viewing material that is sexually objectifying can contribute to body dissatisfaction, eating disorders, low self-esteem, depressive affect, and even physical health problems in high-school-aged girls and in young women.

In addition to leading to feelings of shame and anxiety, sexualizing treatment and self-objectification can generate feelings of disgust toward one's physical self. Girls may feel they are "ugly" and "gross" or untouchable.

Supersexualise me

In the past it was often adult women who understood that their bodies were being pulled apart bit by bit and analysed for imperfections and flaws. Women understood the imperative to be sexy, a message shored up by advertising propaganda, which works 'to deny women's humanity, to present them not as whole people but as fetishised, dismembered "bits," as objects' (Gill, 2009).

Now this understanding has come to younger girls, who learn to see that they too are always at risk of failing.

Courtney Martin (2007, p. 1) has noted that many girls say they would rather be hit by a truck than be fat. I know of a fit and healthy five-year-old who won't go swimming because, she says, people would laugh at her and say she's too fat. Eight-year-old girls are admitted to hospital with eating disorders. Schoolgirls develop ranking systems on the basis of 'hotness,' resulting in guaranteed misery for the girl with the lowest ranking. Cyberspace has become a central arena for bullying where girls are universally judged. Many feel they are dying a social death and disintegrate emotionally. For some, emotional disintegration leads to physical disintegration with the ultimate tragic outcome.

Girls internalise the body critiquing messages of shows like *Extreme Makeover* and *America's Next Top Model* and its Australian version. The program *Ten Years Younger in Ten Days* puts couples in glass boxes at Sydney's Circular Quay so that 100 passers-by can tell us what they think of their looks. 'She looks like she just gave up,' commented one viewer (Channel 7, May 12, 2009) before the transformation begins, and the women have their faces pumped full of botox and fillers until they look like chipmunks with cheeks so plump they can hardly talk, their feet stuffed into heels so high they can barely walk.

The main character of *Twilight*, Stephenie Meyer's book series (2005-2008) and blockbuster film consumed by girls around the world, yearns to be a vampire like her romantic hero Edward. He and his vampire family are impossibly beautiful, 'Greek god' like, with perfect teeth, lips and skin and bodies. They are rich, have the best clothes and drive fast cars. While there are one or two salutary messages in this series—for example, Edward is sexually restrained (OMG!)—the emphasis on physical perfection and its potential impact on millions of young readers cannot be ignored.

English girl Sasha Bennington absorbed today's messages about what constitutes female beauty early:

> Sasha...has a spray tan once a week and a new set of acrylic nails once a month. Her hair is bleached white-blonde and regularly boosted with a set of extensions. She plucks her eyebrows and carefully applies make-up every morning. Her favourite outfit is a white satin boob-tube dress and Stetson hat. *But Sasha isn't a Vegas showgirl—she goes to primary school and only turned 11 last week* [italics in original]. While most children her age have been desperately waiting for the arrival of the new Harry Potter, little Sasha has been hanging on for her heroine Jordan's latest book. She says, 'I'm obsessed with her' (in Ley, 2007).

Sasha's bedroom, the UK *Sun* article tells us, is 'a pink shrine to Playboy, with a Playboy door curtain, satin duvet set, Playboy pillows and pyjamas.' Her mother orders Playboy clothing for her daughter from the USA. For Sasha, the thought of not being pretty is just too awful to contemplate: 'My mum would just call me ugly. Everyone would call me ugly. I wouldn't like that at all.'

Playboy make-up, including 'Tie me to the bedpost blush' and 'Hef's favorite lip gloss' (in colours 'Centerfold Red,' 'Sex Kitten' and 'Playmate Pink') is marketed to girls, along with Playboy doona covers and pencil cases. Girls are wearing the brand of the global sex industry directed by a sleazy 80-year-old man in silk pyjamas and they think it's about cute rabbits. When Hugh Hefner was asked by the *Washington Post* about a growing trend among young girls to wear Playboy-logo clothing and accessories, he replied, 'I don't care if a baby holds up a Playboy bunny rattle' (Sessions Stepp, 2008).

More generally, children's underwear is described as reflecting moods which are 'frisky, seductive or mysteriously alluring' (http://www.jellydeal.co.uk/girls-underwear.html), and padded decorative bras and g-strings are sold in the children's wear sections of department stores. T-shirts for babies include slogans such as 'Breast Fed Baby: Stick around for the show,' 'All daddy wanted was a blow job,' 'Hung like a five year old,' 'F!# the milk, where's the whiskey tits,' 'I tore mummy a new one,' 'I enjoy a good spanking,' and 'I'm too sexy for my diaper.'

What was once considered unthinkable is now ordinary. Children are no longer out of bounds for anything. Pornographic material became pervasive in the public space of adult culture; now it has worked its way into childhood, even into the crib.

The performance model of female sexuality

Everywhere girls are presented with a performance model of female sexuality. They are 'being invited to see themselves not as healthy, active and imaginative girls, but as hot and sassy tweens on the prowl', write Emma Rush and Andrea La Nauze in 'Corporate Paedophilia: Sexualisation of Children in Australia' (2006, p. 23).

In 2008, the Vassarette underwear brand went searching to 'find the most talented female musicians confident enough to perform in their bras' (http://www.thevassarettes.com/, content quoted since removed due to the 'band's' tour ending—but watch out for the 'reunion tour'). Apparently, to sing with a top on means you lack confidence. Emily says, 'Singing in my Vassarette bra makes it even more exciting. I got my first bra when I was 12. Now, I love getting up on that stage in my bra and proving to the world that women are amazing and unstoppable.' And who does she thank for her inspiration? 'That's easy. My Mom. She's the strongest, most beautiful woman I know. She taught me women can love their bodies and be sexy at any bra size. Wearing my RealSexy-DoubleDelight bra on stage makes me understand that more than ever.'

The pornification of young women is carried out under the guise of being in 'her own interest.' Cleverly, this process has become linked with the support of 'good causes' such as care for the environment.

It is becoming more routine for women to be expected to strip off for a good cause. On the cover of the June 2009 issue of *Rolling Stone*, the young Australian supermodel Miranda Kerr is depicted naked and chained to a tree. This is because she wants to save koalas. Most environmentalists seem content to chain themselves to trees with their clothes on—and it certainly helps lessen the chances of a koala scratch or a splinter in the bum. Miranda says she wants to 'make a positive difference…especially for young women' (Moran, 2009).

So, if you're a young woman and you want to make a positive difference, get your clothes off. You can't possibly expect to change the world fully clothed. Are girls included in important causes and debates only for the contribution they can make in 'sexing up' the issue?

And if you're a young woman working for the man, it's not a bad idea to wear a g-string in the office. In a 2006 article in *The Guardian* entitled 'Today's ultimate feminists are the chicks in crop tops,' Kate Taylor points out the advantages of wearing the thong: it will cause men in the office to 'waste whole afternoons staring at your bottom, placing bets on whether you're wearing underwear.'

You should let them do so, Taylor writes, because you can 'use that time to take over the company' while they are distracted (http://www.guardian.co.uk/commentisfree/2006/mar/23/comment.gender).

Music video clips present women in highly sexualised ways, often as adornments, decorations and sexual play-things. A 2009 clip featuring Ciara and Justin Timberlake, *Love Sex Magic*, depicts multiple scenes of Ciara presenting her backside to Timberlake. He is seated and fully clothed. She is on the ground, backside in the air or legs spread. At one point he spanks her. A black woman, Ciara is also shown in a tiger stripe body suit behind bars as if she were a caged jungle animal, and with a chain on her neck pulled by Timberlake, bringing to mind slavery (http://www.youtube.com/watch?v=zTYT-SiZeFo).

The enmeshing of sex industry practices throughout the culture can be observed in the rise of 'sexting,' where teens and even pre-teens exchange sexual images of themselves via mobile phones. In a 2008 survey by the US National Campaign to Prevent Teen and Unplanned Pregnancy, one out of five teens reported that they have 'electronically sent, or posted online, nude or semi-nude pictures or video of themselves' (www.thenationalcampaign.org/sextech/). Girls as young as thirteen send explicit photos of themselves to others. A survey by *Girlfriend* magazine found four in ten readers had been asked to take a nude photo and forward it (Saurine, 2009; see also 'Alarm at teenage "sexting" traffic,' Bittersby, 2008).

Added to—and further fuelling—all these trends is the frequency of sex-based stunts in the public domain we all share. As an example of just how common this has become, on May 6, 2009, male radio announcers on 2Day FM radio in Sydney (in a show syndicated around the country) held a competition in the station office to see who could masturbate the fastest and who had the largest sperm count. They were each given a porn magazine and sent to the cordoned off toilets for the competition. Female host

Jackie O, whose husband took part, cut and pasted photos of her head onto the female porn stars' bodies to 'help' him.

When the competition is over, one of the men wipes his 'sticky' hand in Jackie O's hair. Her co-host Kyle is declared the winner, having produced the most sperm in the fastest time. He is very proud of himself. The photo gallery on the 2Day FM website declared, 'See Jackie get a hairful, take a closer look at Geoff's shirt after the incident…there is a definite stain!! And see Kyle finish first!' (http://www.2dayfm.com.au/shows/kyleandjackieo/highlights/sperm-test).

All this on daytime radio. This is the wallpaper against which women and girls have to live—and the wallpaper against which we try to raise boys of character and respect. And we're supposed to be blasé about it.

Body image despair, beauty rituals, breast implants, brazilians

The sexualisation of girls has seen a rise in beauty rituals and a desire for cosmetic surgery at ever younger ages. Disordered eating is on the rise. A 2006 National Youth Cultures of Eating Study (O'Dea, 2007) found that close to twenty per cent of adolescent Australian girls use fasting for two or more days to lose weight. Another thirteen per cent use vomiting. Others rely on slimming pills, chewing but not swallowing food, smoking, and laxative abuse, as found in this study. One in four twelve-year-old girls in Australia would like to have cosmetic surgery (AAP, August 12, 2007). A *Sunday Mail* (Brisbane) investigation in 2008 reported a twenty per cent increase in inquiries from teenage girls for plastic surgery (in Giles, 2008).

A Queensland surgeon was quoted in the *Sunday Mail* report as saying that between five and ten per cent of young women want to look like the former *Big Brother* contestant Krystal Forscutt (in Giles, 2008). Cosmetic surgery practitioners are cashing in on the body angst of girls and women, with growing numbers of teenage girls having breast implants. A *Cosmopolitan* report noted:

> Young women—many still in their early teens—are lining up in record numbers to get fake breasts…When Amy, a beautiful 18-year-old, performed well in her final year of high school, her parents threw her a graduation party. But to really reward her for a job well done, they bought her a special gift: fake breasts. "I just felt as though I wouldn't be complete without them," says Amy, who went from an A-cup to a C-cup…"I could have gotten a new car, but I'd much rather have bigger breasts. Now," she says, "I feel like a real woman" (in de la Cruz, 2004, p. 129).

Thanks to the globalisation of the body-beautiful mantra, similar things are happening in almost every part of the world. A feature in *India Today* opens:

> Dating her classmate was fun for Priyanka Sood, but keeping up with his demands was not. After a year, he began pressuring her to improve her vital statistics because she didn't look "hot" enough in her halters and tube tops. So, at 16, she went under the surgeon's scalpel to enhance her bust because she could not deal with the rejection. While admitting that she underwent a serious surgery at such a raw age, this teenager has absolutely no regrets. Now 18, Sood believes she is more confident than she was at 16 and besides, "I look great in my swim suit," she says (in Bhupta and Pai, 2007, p. 57).

The makers of a UK Channel 4 documentary 'The Sex Education Show v Pornography,' screened in March 2009, showed photographs of ten pairs of breasts to a group of boys from Sheringham High School in Norfolk. According to a *Guardian* article (Campbell, March 30, 2009):

> All say the most attractive are the ones that have been surgically enhanced. Alarmingly, a posse of their female

classmates says the same thing. Both sexes are unimpressed with normal breasts, which—unlike porn stars' silicone-boosted chests—are often not symmetrical and sit down, not up.

Almost half the girls at Sheringham High School were unhappy with their breasts.

Even small children get the message that the real thing just isn't good enough. *My Beautiful Mommy*, a 2008 book by a Florida plastic surgeon, Michael Salzhauer, is written to explain mummy's new makeover. The book's front cover shows mummy in body hugging pants and snug top, enhancing her pert new breasts. Surrounding her is pink stardust, as though she's been touched by a fairy. What girl doesn't find sparkly stardust appealing? Maybe the magic cosmetic surgeon will visit them too one day? A more fitting title would be, 'If mommy's not good enough maybe I'm not either?'

The nerve-paralysing poison, botox, is being pitched to young women as a 'preventative' against wrinkles. Teenage girls ashamed of their pubic hair are also subjecting themselves to brazilian waxes. A thirteen-year-old girl I know received photos of hair-free genitals on her mobile phones from schoolboys who asked her when she was going to get hers 'done.'

Because of the way pornography shapes expectations, young people are increasingly repulsed by a woman's unmodified body. To take another example from the Channel 4 documentary mentioned above, when the program-makers showed boys and girls an image of a woman with pubic hair, they gasped.

Girl.com.au is a Melbourne-based website allegedly devoted to 'empowering girls.' In 2008, the site's home page was promoting brazilian waxing along with *High School Musical Two*, *Playschool*, Fisher-Price smart toys for pre-schoolers and Barbie Princess dolls. The site's creators wrote, 'Nobody really likes hair in their private regions and it has a childlike appeal. Men love it, and are eternally curious about it.' The creators seemed to have no problem combining waxing, men and childlike appeal in the one sentence.[2]

The disempowering adults at Girl.com.au seemed to think it a fine thing for girls and women to regularly submit themselves to a painful process in order to imitate the genital regions of pre-pubescent girls and to please 'curious' men. Promoting waxing to young girls leads them to despise their natural bodies, increasing their angst by making them feel there is something wrong with them for preferring to avoid hot wax on their body's most delicate regions.

A *Philadelphia Magazine* article (Denny, 2008) describes mothers taking their pre-pubescent daughters to salons for beauty treatments. Some mothers requested waxing for their daughters even though there was nothing to remove. A paediatrician quoted in the article quipped that she was thinking of writing a book called *Where has all the pubic hair gone?*—she almost never sees it.

The Lolita Effect

We see in these examples a phenomenon identified by M. Gigi Durham as the *Lolita Effect*, that is, 'the distorted and delusional set of myths about girls' sexuality that circulates widely in our culture and throughout the world' (2008, p. 12). Girls are encouraged 'to flirt with a decidedly grown-up eroticism and sexuality.'

One mother described the impact of these myths on her thirteen-year-old daughter, in a poignant letter to *The Age* (Melbourne):

> I AM THE mother of a 13-year-old girl. She is not overly developed, she does not wear makeup, she is aware of her burgeoning sexuality, but a little daunted by it and curious of it. Whenever I go out with her—be it to a shopping centre, a walk down the road or picking her up from school—she is gawked at, wolf-whistled and stared at by men usually aged in their 20s and 30s.

2   Under pressure, the gushing endorsement of pubic hair ripping was removed from their website.

OBJECTIFYING.... girls, animals, the earth

It doesn't matter that she is standing with her mother. They do not hesitate for a second. They wave and gesticulate while she's sitting in the car next to me. Her girlfriends also suffer this indignity.

I believe this is the result of the sexualisation of children that some men think it's fine to lust after them—and not just fine, but acceptable. It doesn't matter if they see revulsion, fear or confusion because they're looking at these girls' faces. The girls are totally objectified...I don't think it even enters these men's heads that it is not only offensive, but frightening to attract naked lust when you are only 13 (Morris, 2007, p. 8).

It was also considered acceptable for images of a little girl depicted childishly yet with make-up and adult jewellery, to be mixed in with images of torture porn in Australia's leading arts magazine. Critics were told they just didn't understand art. In 2008, this young girl featured on the cover and, reclining naked and made-up, on the inside pages of *Art Monthly Australia*. The issue was intended by the editors as a defence of Bill Henson and his photos of pre-pubescent boys and girls, which had sparked significant debate in Australia (see Bray, this volume). The girl in *Art Monthly* was positioned alongside images of semi-naked and bound women with protruding sex organs, a Japanese schoolgirl trussed in rope and suspended with her skirt raised to reveal her underwear, and an image of a woman being bound with the tentacles of an octopus as it performs oral sex on her (Tankard Reist, 2008).

In so many ways, little girls are growing up in the shadow cast by a pornographic vision of sexuality.

Girl selling

In the year 2000, the International Labour Organisation estimated there were 1.8 million children being exploited in the commercial sex industry (ILO, 2008, p. 2). UNICEF's report *State of the World's Children* for 2006 gives an estimate of two million children now enslaved in this trade (ILO, 2008, p. 2).

The children are put to work in brothels, massage parlours and strip clubs. They are used to produce pornography. Violence and abuse are part of their daily lives. Writing this now, I can see the faces of the ethnic Vietnamese girls I met in Cambodia, being cared for by the Christian organisation which had rescued them from unspeakable terrors. Small human fodder for the facilitation of masturbation by men of all ethnicities, they suffered physical and mental injuries. One had a colostomy bag. Another had surgery to repair internal damage. Another was mentally beyond repair. Some of the girls were used to make pornographic films, which could be purchased for $US1.50 only blocks from where they were now living. Two village girls were about to travel to Los Angeles to testify against their American abuser, a daunting prospect that their carers feared might add further trauma to their already scarred selves.

This is the ultimate outworking of the sexualising of girls. M. Gigi Durham describes the links between sexualisation and girl selling:

> Dressed up in the clothing made cute and seemingly innocuous by the Bratz, the Pussycat Dolls, and the juniors' styles bedecked with sleazy slogans, child sex workers are living embodiments of Lolita. They take the implications of the Lolita Effect to the ultimate conclusion: that young girls' bodies are an appropriate element of sexual commerce. The scale of this enterprise is monstrous…The children involved are as young as toddlers, sometimes even babies…[Children] are garmented in the skimpy skirts, bustiers, thong underwear, and transparent tops of the Lolita Effect (2008, p. 205).

[handwritten margin note: The marketing power of these issues]

These links between sexualisation and the selling of girls become even more sinister in Third World contexts, where the sexual exploitation of very young girls, so often for the benefit of western male tourists, is on open display. As Durham further notes:

> Peter Landesman of the *New York Times Magazine* describes child prostitutes in Mexico 'in stilettos and spray-on-tight neon vinyl and satin or skimpy leopard-patterned outfits.' The *New York Times* journalist Nicholas Kristof writes about 'Chai Hour' in Phnom Penh, Cambodia, where young teenage girls 'in skimpy white outfits' stand in glass cages to be rented for sex. An *Economist* story depicts young Vietnamese girl prostitutes in heavy makeup and Gucci high-heeled sandals. Lisa Ling's documentary *Slave Girls of India* shows a madam in an Indian brothel bragging about her 'baby beauties.' It's no wonder, then, that when we see these outfits in the children's sections of department stores, or in Halloween costume catalogs, or in media targeted to kids, some of us are creeped out (2008, p. 206).

In the transmission of messages to girls about their role in providing round-the-clock sexual come-ons, the media acts in many ways as a de facto pimp for the prostitution and pornography industries.

The impact of pornography: girls as service stations for boys

We don't have to travel overseas to see the way the Lolita image is traded as sexual merchandise. Adult sex magazines encouraging sex with young girls, rape and incest, are easily accessible in corner stores, milkbars and petrol stations in Australia (and elsewhere), although thanks to women like Julie Gale, at fewer petrol stations than previously (see Gale, this volume). The young women in these magazines are supposed to be over eighteen. In some cases, this is questionable. But even if they are over eighteen, the models are often posed and styled to look much younger, with toys, braces, pigtails and other accoutrements of childhood (Tankard

Reist, 2008). In the words of Pamela Paul (2005, p. 198), 'the desire for a child and the desire for a childlike woman blur and overlap' in these materials.

Pornography has become the handbook of sex education for many boys. An estimated 70 per cent of boys have seen pornography by the age of twelve and 100 per cent by the age of fifteen (Scobie, 2007, p. 35). Girls are also increasingly exposed to pornographic images. In her research for *Sex Lives of Australian Teenagers*, Australian author Joan Sauers found that 53.5 per cent of girls twelve and under in Australia have seen pornography, 97 per cent by the age of sixteen (2007, p. 80).[3]

Fourteen-year-old girls are even looking to pornography for guidance. 'I just copied what i had seen from porn, he enjoyed it,' a girl of this age told Sauers (2007, p. 53). The main aim seems to be the boy's enjoyment, even when a girl is in pain. Some girls in Sauers' study reported being in pain but allowing their partners to continue in order to make them happy; the girls 'put up with it' to make sex enjoyable for their boyfriends (in Sauers, 2007, p. 57). They were treated like crash-test dummies, not intimate partners. Another girl wrote: 'it really hurt, I bled, but I let him keep going, he seemed happy. i really regretted it after doing it, but there wasn't much I could do, I just felt way too young and that it was too early.' This girl was aged 13 (in Sauers, 2007, p. 57).

Even magazines that are not explicitly pornographic in intent often promote a view of girls as service stations for boys.[4] A 2007 issue of *Dolly*—read by girls not yet in their teens—contained a section entitled 'OMG my boyfriend wants me to...', followed by three sexual acts: 'Give him "head",' 'Have anal sex' and 'Give him a hand job' (*Dolly,* August 2007, p. 141). *Dolly* gave a clinical

---

3 More statistics on young people's exposure to porn can be found at: http://www.enough.org/inside.php?id=2UXKJWRY8. See also Flood and Hamilton, 'Regulating youth access to pornography,' Australia Institute, 2003.

4 The expression 'girls are like a service station for boys' comes from Liz Perle, vice president of Common Sense Media. Girls in these sexual relationships are the 'pleasure providers' (in Durham, 2008, p. 55).

description of each act. There was no mention that the girl might be physically or psychologically hurt or violated, or that it might be a crime depending on their respective ages.

Girls are expected to possess a sexual knowingness at increasingly younger ages. They learn not the desire for the other, but the desire to be desired (Wolf, 1991, p. 157). Girls who want romance must pay for it with sexual tokens. This is the advice for those looking to be romanced by their partner given in the Q&A section 'Paging Doctor Love' from *Famous Weekly* (June 11, 2007, p. 56):

> *Q:* How can I get my partner to do more romantic things?
>
> *A:* Promise him wild sex in return for romance and be sure to deliver—then keep rewarding him like that.

The magazine then goes on to dispense advice to romance-seeking women who aren't enthusiastic deliverers of oral sex.

Ten years ago, in *The Whole Woman*, Germaine Greer was already observing the way magazines endorsed a role for girls as pleasure providers. Her words apply even more today:

> The cynicism of the merchandisers of bad-girl culture is perfectly reflected in the brutal lay-out of girls' magazines…From them the emerging girl learns that the only life worth living is a life totally out of control, disrupted by debt, disordered eating, drunkenness, drugs and casual sex…The little girl who pores over this sinister muck has no way of knowing whether the life described is real or not…they [tell] them that any sexual interaction is better than none; that a cool girl gives hand–jobs and head, fakes orgasm and has less flesh on her limbs than a sparrow (Greer, 1999, pp. 313–314).

The rhetoric of empowerment becomes the face of degradation.

Wendy Shalit puts the point well in *Girls Gone Mild*, in writing about nineteen-year-old Debbie who appeared in a 'scene' for a *Girls Gone Wild* video. Debbie was upset about 'not doing it' right for the camera; she just couldn't get excited. Shalit observes: 'Debbie is publicly sexual while remaining utterly alienated from her own sexuality' (2007, p. xii).

No matter what spin is put on it, however, degradation is not empowerment. To apply a question asked by Ariel Levy in 2005: 'Why is this the "new feminism" and not what it looks like: the old objectification?' (Levy, 2005, p. 81).

Pornography is also used to groom children for sex, normalising graphic depictions of sex acts in a child's psyche. Growing numbers of children are even acting out on other children what they have seen in porn.[5]

It was reported in 2008 that a group of six-year-old boys ran a 'sex club' at a Brisbane primary school, threatening girls who refused to comply. The *Courier Mail* reported the case of a seven-year-old girl performing oral sex on a boy during lunchtime: 'The witness said the boy had menaced the girl and threatened her with violence' (September 13, 2008).

Pornography presents women as live sex toys, and men as wild and predatory animals. It makes the abuse of women inviting and erotic. Pornography's scripts ('*command the bitches*') are being acted out in real life in Australian cities and towns, involving younger and younger boys and girls. We are seeing more of the male sexual bonding rituals in which girls are seen as conquests, there to be degraded. Kerry Carrington, writing of the murder of fourteen-year-old Leigh Leigh at a party in Newcastle, Australia, described these rituals of sexual conquest as the 'product of a social chemistry

---

5   The Ninth Australasian Conference on Child Abuse and Neglect in November 2003 was told by staff from the Child at Risk Assessment Unit at the Canberra Hospital that exposure to X-rated pornography was a significant factor in children younger than ten-years-old sexually abusing other children. In the first six months of 2003, 48 children under ten were identified as having engaged in sexually abusive acts. Access to graphic sexual images had shaped the trend (Stanley et al., 2003). In the UK, the number of cases in which children received court orders or warnings for sex offences has jumped by twenty per cent in the past three years; experts say that the youth behaviour has been changed by ready access to sexual imagery on the internet (*This is London,* March 3, 2007).

forged on a dangerous cocktail of mateship and machismo' (Carrington, 1998, p. 163), arguing that 'Girls are the pawns in this ritual demonstration of sexual vigour' (1998, p. 161).

In July 2007, a thirteen-year-old girl was assaulted in toilet blocks and on a rooftop in a Sydney suburb. She was penetrated vaginally and orally by seven boys. The course taken by the assault followed the classic plot line of an average porn film in which one girl is surrounded by many men in a planned attack; it was as if the boys had taken their instructions directly from porn. The boys had cameras at the ready to record the violation and to post on YouTube as home made porn: after all, what's the use of assaulting a woman if you can't brag about your conquest later? Too many young men have become not only consumed by porn but have even taken to manufacturing it at home using their mobiles and computers.

The boys waiting their 'turn' in this attack told the girl to 'smile like you're enjoying it,' just as women in porn are told to look like they're having the time of their lives.[6]

One report of the attack claimed that the boys forced the girl to 'take off her clothes and watched one another violate her, causing her to bleed' (Alexander, 2009). Lawyers representing four of the seven attackers told the NSW District Court that a 'lack of sex education' was one of the reasons they did it (in Scheikowski, 2009). However, it wasn't a lack of sex education that was at work here; rather, the actions of the boys suggest that their sex education through porn was very thorough indeed. What they lacked was an education in humanity, common decency and respect. It's as if we are witnessing the death of feeling or empathy for another's suffering.

This attack had overtones of another assault in Werribee, Victoria, in which a sixteen-year-old girl with an intellectual impairment was forced by a gang of boys to expose her breasts and perform oral

---

6   Some ex-porn performers talk about being beaten if they didn't smile (see MacKinnon and Dworkin, 1998).

sex on them. They urinated on her, torched her hair, threatened to shave her—and after, sold the DVDs they had made of the assault for $5 each to their school mates (Medew, 2008). In the western Melbourne suburb, the view that many expressed was that the boys were just 'having a bit of fun' (Robinson, 2006, p. 3).

Kerry Carrington's words are painfully apt in so many cases of sexual assault against girls, including against Indigenous Australian girls, who don't know they have a right to say 'no' (see McLellan, this volume). Carrington wrote that very few girls who are the targets of sexual assault

> …possess the necessary legal knowledge or language to describe themselves as having been sexually assaulted without their consent. We can expect that this is especially so when they grow up in an environment where a degree of sexual intimidation is normal—where sex is expected, where sexual autonomy is not respected, where girls who do say *no*, are threatened, abused or ostracised, and where the pretext of romance is a lure for entrapment (1998, p. 161).

Coercion, force and unwanted sex

A 2008 report by an Australian anti-violence organisation, the White Ribbon Foundation, cited research showing that one in seven girls and young women aged between twelve and twenty have experienced rape or sexual assault. Among girls who have ever had sex, 30.2 per cent of Year 10 girls and 26.6 per cent of Year 12 girls have experienced unwanted sex. Fourteen per cent of young women said that a boyfriend had tried to force them to have sex, and six per cent said a boyfriend had physically forced them to have sex (White Ribbon Foundation, 2008, p. 18).

Ann Evans (2000) reports on a study in Adelaide that found that 32 per cent of young men aged 14 to 26 believe that it is acceptable to force a woman to have sex under certain circumstances. A study by the University of Western Australia published in 2009 found that coercion was a common reason for premature and unwanted first experiences of sexual intercourse (Skinner, 2009).

According to the Coalition Against Trafficking in Women (Australia), 'The increasing incidence…of boys perpetrating sexual crimes against women and girls in Australia might be an indication of a trend toward a more callous attitude in men's sexual treatment of women created through the normalisation of the sex industry' (CATWA 2008; see also Farley, this volume). It is not difficult to find even extreme examples of male violence these days.

Something that especially saddened me in research for this book and in my interaction with girls at schools and elsewhere, was the way they are treated in their everyday lives. I fear that we have gone backward. In a Canberra school in 2008, teachers told me of boys groping the girls in the classroom, even during class and with the teacher present. Girls were aware that male students were spending lunchtimes downloading porn on their mobile phones, which added to their sense of threat.

In almost every group of girls with whom I talk, I am told stories about verbal abuse, harassment and even sexual assault including rape. When I ask them why they don't report the matter to police, they respond by saying things like: why make a fuss?; it hasn't just happened to them but to lots of girls; what if they were blamed or weren't believed; it's something they just have to put up with. They also fear retribution. In the poignant words of a fifteen-year-old girl in *Sex Lives of Australian Teenagers*: 'I've had friends who were raped, sexually abused, i've been molested, it's just really sad to feel disconnected from your own self' (in Sauers, 2007, p. 112).

Violence: the new sexy

We are also seeing the normalisation of male violence against women: violence and sex are merging.

Increasing numbers of young people are playing games featuring graphic sex and violence, in which the female characters are prostituted, attacked or raped. Some of us worked to ban a Japanese rape-simulator game that was based on players raping a mother and her two young daughters, one of whom was ten and carrying a teddy bear. The website described the game as 'a new type [of] molesting game with more beautiful 3D images…Players can get the new excitement like never before.'[7] We succeeded in outlawing its download in Australia.[8]

A March 2008 episode of *America's Next Top Model*, shown in a 6.30 pm Sunday slot on Channel 10 before *Australian Idol*, featured a 'crime scenes' segment (shot in Australia) in which the aspiring model had to pretend she had been brutally murdered. The model who looked the sexiest in death was the winner of the episode. The categories were: 'pushed off rooftop,' 'organs stolen,' 'electrocuted,' 'stabbed,' 'decapitated' and so on. Girls, you must look sexy all the time—even when you're dead.

Continuing the murdered woman theme, a European clothing and shoe company, Loula, put together an ad campaign in 2008 featuring murdered women. To celebrate the opening of the company's new store in Melbourne, a full page glossy advertisement ran in *Harper's Bazaar* depicting a murdered woman in the boot of a car. The ad, in an issue out just in time for International Women's Day, was pulled after outrage expressed by women's anti-violence groups. In 2005, a Melbourne woman had been left for dead in the boot of her car for five days after an attempt on

---

7 'Government must act immediately to end access to downloadable gang rape game,' Women's Forum Australia, February 25, 2009, http://womensforumaustralia.com/images/pressreleases/090225%20downloadable%20rape%20game.pdf. Anti-violence activists in the US have received death threats for their attempts to ban the game (personal communication, May 13, 2009). As I finalised this introduction, the *Sydney Morning Herald* reported (June 6, 2009) that a Japanese software industry body had decided to ban computer games in which players simulate sexual violence against women: http://www.smh.com.au/news/home/technology/japan-bans-sexual-torture-software/2009/06/06/1244234406067.html

8 Richard Fraser, Manager, Content Assessment Section, Australian Communications and Media Authority, email communication, April 7, 2009, re online content complaint (Reference 2009000101/ACMA-197982360).

her life, mere blocks from where the store was to open (Tankard Reist, 2009).

Girls and women are pitted against each other through sexualisation. Ads for *Skins She* sportswear, popular with young women, purvey women-hating messages such as, 'Get a body to die for…and watch other women line up to make your funeral arrangements.' Other slogans include, 'Get the body every other woman would love. To spit on,' and '…for legs that will feel like heaven. And that's exactly where other women will want to send you.'

How far we haven't come

Young women write to me about the pressures they feel in a sexualised culture. Nadia, who is nineteen and lives in regional Victoria, wrote, 'No wonder females today think they are not good enough for men, because men have these bizarre standards that they have to have a "sexy" girl with a good body that makes them look good.' Nadia wrote that after her relationship broke up, 'I was abused with text messages that I was a fat tree stump and that I needed to go onto a treadmill for five days straight in order to look good. He was a pig who degraded me so bad, who constantly judged me on my appearance' (personal correspondence, June 16, 2008, used with permission).

Kate, a Canberra teenager, wrote: 'The feelings of worthlessness and loss of self that I developed while with the last two boyfriends were more than I could bear and I spent my life trying to please them by "perfecting" my image.' Kate was hospitalised for two months with an eating disorder. On leaving hospital, and in Year 11, she was confronted with 'Posters of semi-clad models staring me in the face telling me to conform to the ideals I had spent two months in hospital trying to dispel from my mind. Certain words screamed louder. Skinny. Diet. Size. Shape. It was EVERYWHERE! The world seemed to be throwing my eating disorder ammunition I couldn't combat' (personal correspondence, June 14, 2008, used with permission).

And Tara from Perth said:

> I am 19 years of age and have a close group of male friends, and my very close group of girl friends. Most of these girls have nearly perfect Body-Mass Indexes. They are all smart and kind and none of them are ugly. Their faces however are NOT anywhere near like a model. When asking my male friends...their opinions of my friends can be summed up in phrases such as 'Ew' 'oh-my-god-kill-me-now' and 'I was expecting bad but this is...' and I know that it is not just my friends. In 4 past workplaces, High School and University, the trend has been the same...most of the guys I know are cruel in their judging of women (personal correspondence, February 12, 2008, used with permission).

Young women like Nadia, Kate and Tara have a desperate need to have their voices heard above the noise of a sexualised body worshipping culture.

Getting Real

As the essays in *Getting Real: Challenging the Sexualisation of Girls* show, you don't have to be embittered and in need of a new body to care about the sexualisation of girls in the media and popular culture.

Dr Emma Rush summarises the global research on the evidence for sexualisation and the risks of sexualisation which undermine the strong social norms that prohibit sexual interest in children. Together with Andrea La Nauze, Emma Rush kick-started the debate on sexualisation of children in Australia, in two key reports for the Australia Institute in 2006. (In her chapter, Julie Gale reveals material discovered in a Freedom of Information request that validates the Institute's claims about the use of underage sexualised models by a major Australian retailer.)

Author and publisher Maggie Hamilton, drawing on her extensive work in the field, gives a solid overview of the issues facing young girls and the impacts on their mental, emotional and physical health.

Dr Lauren Rosewarne, author of the finely researched *Sex in Public: Women, Outdoor Advertising and Public Policy* (2007) describes how women continue to be portrayed in advertising in sexualised ways. As Rosewarne asks in her book, why is it that if a man were to put up a pin-up of a naked or semi-naked woman in his office this would be considered sexual harassment, but advertisers put up giant billboards in the public space with sexual depictions of women with little to stop them (Rosewarne, 2007, p. 3)?

Professor Louise Newman speaks in the authoritative voice of a medical professional who has worked at the coalface with troubled girls.

Public intellectual Dr Clive Hamilton writes a thoughtful and reflective piece on how young women are sold out by a hypersexualised culture which expects them to be constantly sexually available. He observes that where once teenage sexual activity was a sign of rebellion, now it is those who refrain who have become the dissenters. 'This refusal signals independence of mind…Once only the timid and compliant held back from sex; now it is the confident and courageous who refrain…"Bad" no longer signifies rebellion but compliance.'

Selena Ewing who authored the cutting edge magazine-style research paper *Faking It* (Women's Forum Australia, 2007), revisits and elaborates on the paper's findings about body image issues and young women.

Author and academic Dr Abigail Bray provides important commentary on photographer Bill Henson's exhibition, exploring how labelling of critics as zealots and fanning the flames of 'moral panic' shut down legitimate and necessary debate.

Author of a number of books on prostitution and trafficking and recognised as a global authority on the subject, Dr Melissa Farley makes a compelling argument that 'trained by popular western culture, girls learn to present a hypersexualised, prostitution-like version of themselves to the world.'

My long time co-worker in many projects, biologist, author and women's health researcher Dr Renate Klein, authors an essay on how the medicalisation of girls goes hand in hand with the sexualisation of girls.

Long time women's advocate, author and psychotherapist Dr Betty McLellan situates activism against the sexualisation of girls within the broader context of advocacy for women and girls in the women's movement. McLellan demonstrates how off the mark it is to interpret the 'sexual revolution' as a great leap forward in women's quest for equality.

Steve Biddulph, whose writings have assisted many parents in raising boys, offers personal reflections on girls and the stifling, life-sucking culture in which they are being raised: 'In a piecemeal, cumulative way, this is invading and tarnishing girls' vision of themselves, making it almost impossible to put together a positive and integrated sense of self.'

Tania Andrusiak, author of *Adproofing Your Kids* (2009), challenges all women to make changes at a personal level, especially in the way they treat each other. Tania calls for supportive alliances and friendships across the differences that women have. 'If more women reassured each other that they had companions on this battlefield, if we decided to create a supportive sisterhood, if we chose to give each other a break and stop competing, how much easier would it be?'

Getting Real ends with the inspiring contribution of comedian and founder of Kids Free 2B Kids Julie Gale, whose appearances at events dressed as a cross between a Bratz doll/Pussycat doll/ Playboy bunny have become almost legendary. Julie shows what one woman's activism can achieve, stirs us into action and gives us hope for change. Her chapter seemed the perfect note on which to end this collection.

This book is not only about girls. It has to be about women as well. We make no apology for that. Girls become women, and the way each is treated will have an impact on the other. It is a continuum: just as women are infantilised in pornography, little girls are adultified for male pleasure. We can't address the sexualisation of girls in isolation. If the sexualisation of girls has become normalised, so has the sexualisation of women. Children won't be freed from this harmful culture unless women are as well. This book calls for a re-personalisation of girls—and women—in which we recognise that all are unique and deserving of respect. The same applies to boys and men. We all need to be re-sensitised to the importance of being treated with respect and dignity.

Identifying real values, resisting dehumanisation: a new movement for women and girls

A culture obsessed with exhibitionist sexualised display and climbing as high as you can on a sexual hierarchy limits the freedom of girls to explore all the other facets of their lives. The American Psychological Association makes the vital point that 'sexualization practices may function to keep girls "in their place" as objects of sexual attraction and beauty, significantly limiting their free thinking and movement in the world' (APA TSG 2007, p. 22).

Girls should be rewarded for thinking for themselves, exploring meaning and values and making a mark in the world that goes beyond the airhead cult of celebrity and fashion. They can be engineers, scientists, lawyers and politicians. They can be hairdressers, teachers, army officers, journalists and mothers. They are valued in boardrooms, universities, the media, sport, banking, disaster relief and international diplomacy. But just when it seems we have made so much progress, young women are told to let their bodies do the talking:

> *Shush girl shut your lips,*
> *Do the Hellen Keller and talk with your hips*
> —'Don't Trust Me' by 3OH!3

3OH!3 not only gets her name wrong (it's Helen Keller). The group also seems not to care how disrespectful their song is in appropriating the name of such a heroine as Keller, a visually impaired woman who overcame many obstacles; an advocate for women and people with disabilities, a militant suffragist who not only didn't talk with her hips, but was completely unconcerned with outward appearances.

A young artist I know who struggles with an eating disorder and exercise addiction expressed it this way: 'I feel it's essential that not only girls, but women, are able to identify the real values we should nurture, and the deeply dishonest images and ideas we are fed' (personal correspondence, July 22, 2007).

Girls need to be able to discern what is good and valuable and dismiss the rubbish.

They need to be nourished physically, of course, but also spiritually and emotionally, to help build resilience and be able to navigate their way through a tough world.

The world needs girls who desire to be whole, well rounded, citizens of the world—and adults who will facilitate this. We need to insist they (and all of us) deserve better. We all need a world that makes true human development possible.

There's a lot of dark material in this book. However, there is hope. A new movement is taking shape against objectification and sexualisation, one that goes beyond the usual polarities of left and right and religious and other differences. A diverse collection of organisations and individuals are coming together to agitate for the dignity and worth of girls and women, using everything from culture-jamming grassroots activism to more formal lobbying and advocacy.

This movement presents great hope. It is helping girls see that succumbing to the demands and dictates of popular culture, and adhering to pornified roles and behaviours, causes them to live limited and constricted lives. May this book provide strength, solidarity and resolve to this new movement, for the benefit of girls, boys—and all of us.

References

AAP (2007) 'Cosmetic cuts a goal for girls: survey', AAP August 12.

Alexander, Harriet (2009) 'Schoolboys film sex attack on girl', *The Age*, Melbourne, January 29, http://www.theage.com.au/national/schoolboys-film-sex-attack-on-girl-20090129-7sph.html

American Psychological Association (2007) *Report of the APA task force on the sexualization of girls*, Washington DC, available at www.apa.org/pi/wpo/sexualization.html

Bhupta, Malini and Aditi Pai (2007) 'No Kidding,' *India Today*, June 25, pp. 51–57.

Bittersby, Lucy (2008) 'Alarm at teenage 'sexting' traffic' *The Age*, Melbourne, July 10, p. 3, http://www.theage.com.au/national/alarm-at-teenage-sexting-traffic-20080709-3clg.html

Bottrell, Dorothy and Gabrielle Meagher (Eds) (2008) *Communities and Change: Selected Papers*. Sydney University Press, Sydney.

Brumberg, Joan Jacobs (1997) *The Body Project: An Intimate History of American Girls*. Random House, New York.

Campbell, Denis (2009) 'Porn: the new sex education,' *The*

Guardian, London, March 30, http://www.guardian.co.uk/ society/joepublic/2009/mar/30/teenagers-porn-sex-education

Carrington, Kerry (1998) *Who Killed Leigh Leigh?: A Story of Shame and Mateship in An Australian Town*. Random House, Sydney.

Coalition Against Trafficking in Women Australia (2008) Submission to the National Council to Reduce Violence against Women and Children responding to the National Plan to Reduce Violence against Women and Children, July 31.

de la Cruz, Melissa (2004) 'The boob-job epidemic', *Cosmopolitan*, December 1, p. 129.

Denny, Carrie (2008) 'Trend: Pretty Babies,' *Philadelphia Magazine*, March 28 http://www.phillymag.com/articles/ pretty_babies/page1

Durham, M. Gigi (2008) *The Lolita Effect: The Media Sexualisation of Young Girls and What We Can Do About It*. Overlook Press, New York.

Evans, Ann (2000) 'Power and Negotiation: Young women's choices about sex and contraception' *Journal of Population Research*, November, http://findarticles.com/p/articles/mi_ m0PCG/is_2_17/ai_105657390/

Flood, Michael and Clive Hamilton (2003) 'Regulating youth access to pornography.' *Discussion Paper* Number 53, The Australia Institute, Canberra.

Giles Darrell (2008) 'Ban on cosmetic surgery for teens' *Sunday Mail*, Brisbane, April 6, http://www.news.com.au/ couriermail/story/0,23739,23490657-3102,00.html

Gill, Rosalind (2009) 'Supersexualise Me! Advertising and "the midriffs"', in Feona Attwood (Ed) *Mainstreaming Sex: The Sexualisation of Western Culture*. I.B. Taurus, London, http://www.awc.org.nz/userfiles/16_1176775150.pdf

Greer, Germaine (1999) *The Whole Woman*. Transworld Publishers, London.

International Labour Association (2008) 'Commercial sexual exploitation of children and adolescents: The ILO's response' http://www.ilo.org/global/Themes/Forced_Labour/lang—en/docName—WCMS_100740/index.htm

Levy, Ariel (2005) *Female Chauvinist Pigs: Women and the Rise of Raunch Culture*. Free Press, New York.

Ley, Rebecca (2007) 'Girl wants to be next Jordan,' *The Sun* UK, July 24, http://www.thesun.co.uk/sol/homepage/woman/article248748.ece

MacKinnon, Catharine A. and Andrea Dworkin (Eds) (1998) *In Harm's Way: The Pornography Civil Rights Hearings*. Harvard University Press, Cambridge, MA.

Martin, Courtney E. (2007) *Perfect Girls, Starving Daughters: The Frightening New Normalcy of Hating Your Body*. Free Press, New York.

Medew, Julia (2008) 'Werribee father opposed jail for DVD teens' February 1, http://www.theage.com.au/news/national/werribee-father-opposed-jail-for-dvd-teens/2008/01/31/1201714153350.html

Meyer, Stephenie (2006) *Twilight*. Atom, London.

Moran, Jonathon (2009) 'Miranda Kerr goes nude for Rolling Stone and Koalas' *The Daily Telegraph,* Sydney, May 31, http://www.news.com.au/entertainment/story/0,,25564221-10388,00.html

Morris, Deborah (2007) 'Let girls be girls,' *The Age*, Melbourne, November 17, p. 8.

Nine News (2009) 'Technology fuelling sexting craze: study,' May 12, http://news.ninemsn.com.au/technology/812871/technology-fuelling-sexting-craze-study

Ninemsn (2008) 'Six year old boys "ran sex club",' September 13, http://news.ninemsn.com.au/national/630867/trio-of-schoolboys-ran-sex-club

O'Dea, Jennifer (2007) 'Are we OK or are we not?' *Journal of the*

HEIA, 14:3, p. 6.

Paul, Pamela (2005) *Pornified: How Pornography Is Transforming Our Lives, Our Relationships, and Our Families*. Times Books, New York.

Robinson, Natasha (2006) 'DVD just a bit of fun, say students,' *The Australian*, October 26.

Rosewarne, Lauren (2007) *Sex in Public: Women, Outdoor Advertising and Public Policy*, Cambridge Scholars Publishing, Newcastle, UK.

Rush, Emma and Andrea La Nauze (2006) 'Corporate Paedophilia: Sexualisation of children in Australia.' *Discussion Paper* Number 90, The Australia Institute, Canberra, https://www.tai.org.au/documents/downloads/DP90.pdf

Rush, Emma and Andrea La Nauze (2006) 'Letting Children be Children: Stopping the sexualisation of *children* in Australia' *Discussion Paper,* Number 93, The Australia Institute, Canberra

Salzhauer, Michael (2008) *My Beautiful Mommy*. Big Tent Books, Georgia, USA.

Sauers, Joan (2007) *Sex Lives of Australian Teenagers*. Random House Australia, Sydney.

Saurine, Angela (2009) 'The sad truth of Generation Sex' *The Daily Telegraph*, Sydney, February 2, http://www.news.com.au/dailytelegraph/story/0,22049,24992752-5001031,00.html

Scheikowski, Margaret (2009) 'Youths film sex assault on 13yo girl,' *The Brisbane Times*, January 30 http://www.brisbanetimes.com.au/articles/2009/01/30/1232818677095.html

Scobie, Claire (2007) 'Wild Things' *The Bulletin*, February 6, p. 35. http://www.clairescobie.com/journalism/features/On%20Sex%20Lives%20of%20Teenagers_June07%5B2%5D.pdf

Sessions Stepp, Laura (2008) 'Teenage girls buying the bunny' *Washington Post,* April 1, http://www.azcentral.com/style/articles/0711playboy.html

Shalit, Wendy (2007) *Girls Gone Mild: Young women reclaim*

self-respect and find it's not bad to be good. Random House, New York.

Skinner, Rachel (2009) 'New study finds teen girls regret having sex earlier' May 19, http://insciences.org/article.php?article_id=5101

Stanley, Janet, Cassandra Tinning and Katie Kovacs (2003) 'Child Protection and the Internet' *Ninth Australasian conference on child abuse and neglect,* November 24–27 Napcan, Surrey Hills NSW.

Sydney Morning Herald (2009), http://www.smh.com.au/news/home/technology/japan-bans-sexual-torture-softwa re/2009/06/06/1244234406067.html

Tankard Reist, Melinda (2008) 'Incensed About Censorship' *ABC Unleashed*, November 27, http://www.abc.net.au/unleashed/stories/s2429316.htm

Tankard Reist, Melinda (2008) 'Give this ad the boot' *On Line Opinion,* March 2, http://www.onlineopinion.com.au/view.asp?article=7119&page=3

Tankard Reist, Melinda (2008) 'You say dignity, I say torture porn and ne'er the twain shall meet' *Sydney Morning Herald*, July 10, http://www.smh.com.au/news/letters/you-say-dignity-i-say-torture-porn--and-neer-the-twain-shallme et/2008/07/09/1215282921244.html

Taylor, Kate (2006) 'Today's ultimate feminists are the chicks in crop tops' *The Guardian*, London, March 23, http://www.guardian.co.uk/commentisfree/2006/mar/23/comment.gender

This is London (2007) 'Web is blamed for 20 percent leap in sex attacks by children' March 3.

White Ribbon Foundation (2008) *An Assault on Our Future: The Impact of Violence on Young People and Their Relationships* http://www.whiteribbonday.org.au/media/documents/AssaultOnOurFutureFinal.pdf

Wolf, Naomi (1991) *The Beauty Myth*. Vintage, London.

Women's Forum Australia (2009) 'Government must act immediately to end access to downloadable gang rape game' February 25, http://womensforumaustralia.com/images/ pressreleases/090225%20downloadable%20rape%20game.pdf

What are the Risks of Premature Sexualisation for Children?

Emma Rush

It is important to be familiar with what research tells us about the risks of premature sexualisation for children. Why? To defend children's interests against people who claim that premature sexualisation is not a real problem. In fact, both research evidence and expert opinion suggest that premature sexualisation does indeed place children at risk of harm of various kinds.

1 What is sexualisation, and how does it occur?

Sexualisation of children occurs when 'the slowly developing sexuality of children' is moulded 'into stereotypical forms of adult sexuality' (Rush and La Nauze, 2006, p. 1).

This results from two quite different cultural processes, both driven by commercial interests.

The first cultural process has been going on for decades—the use of sex to sell things to, or entertain, adults. To the extent that children are exposed to this, it can affect their slowly developing sexual identity. As advertising and popular culture have become more heavily sexualised (to the point where some scholars speak of the 'pornification' of culture more generally), the impact upon children has increased.

The other cultural process that sexualises children is relatively new. It involves sexualising products being sold specifically for children, and children themselves being presented in images or directed to act in advertisements in ways modelled on adult sexual behaviour (Rush and La Nauze, 2006, p. 1). To describe this process of directly sexualising children, we have adopted a phrase first used by Phillip Adams: 'corporate paedophilia.' Sexualising products are products linked to cultural norms of sexual attractiveness. Such products were previously reserved for teenagers and adults but are now sold directly to girls of primary school age, for example, bras, platform shoes, lip gloss, fake nails, and so on. Advertising for these products shows clearly that they are no longer being sold for 'creative dress-ups' purposes, as they may have been in previous decades. Rather, they are marketed as products to wear on a daily basis, to get 'the look' that is sold to primary school aged children, despite concern from parents and professionals in child health and welfare. What look is that? 'Hot.'

So today's children are not only exposed to hypersexualised adult culture, but are also directly sold the idea that they should look 'hot'—not later, but now. This means that today's children are facing sexualising pressure quite unlike anything faced by children in the past. What risks might children face as a result of such pressure?

2 Risks for children

What kind of evidence is available?

There is broad agreement from experts in children's health and welfare that premature sexualisation places children at risk of a variety of harms (Wigg et al., 2006; Wigg et al., 2007; APA TSG, 2007). However, there is as yet no conclusive evidence for this, such as could be provided by a carefully designed, large scale, longitudinal study.[1] There are several reasons that such conclusive evidence does not yet exist.

The widespread premature sexualisation of children is a relatively new development. Celebrity gossip magazines specifically targeted at primary school girls, which represent a fundamental shift in childhood culture, only began to become widespread after 2000, as did bras and 'bralettes' specifically made for ages four and up. Large scale, longitudinal studies require careful theoretical development as well as substantial funding into the medium term. Only after almost two years of vigorous debate in Australia did a Federal government report into the sexualisation of children in the contemporary media recommend such a study, to be funded by the National Health and Medical Research Council. However, the report also foresaw significant problems in conducting this kind of study, in particular, the breach of family privacy it might entail, and the risk that such a study might itself further contribute to the process of the sexualisation of children and thus increase any consequent harm (SCECA, 2008, sections 3.27–3.29).

So conclusive evidence does not yet exist, and it may not ever be possible to obtain such conclusive evidence due to intrinsic problems in researching this very complex and sensitive area. Yet this does not mean that there is no evidence at all about the harms that premature sexualisation may cause children. Indeed, there is relevant evidence from a range of research studies, as well as expert opinion about the risks premature sexualisation poses to children. The major risks include:

- increased body dissatisfaction;
- development of eating disorders at younger ages;
- increased self-objectification;

---

1   A longitudinal study is one that follows the subjects of the research over a number of years. Such studies can prove causality, for example, that premature sexualisation causes an increase in eating disorders. Studies conducted at a single point in time can only prove association, for example, that children who have a more sexualised self-concept are more likely than those who don't to suffer from an eating disorder.

- disruption to healthy psychological development; and
- contribution to increasing child sexual abuse.

Increased body dissatisfaction

Studies of body image carried out in Australia and in similar countries have now established that girls as young as six to seven years of age:

- desire a thinner ideal body;
- are 'aware of dieting to lose weight';
- are 'beginning to engage in disordered eating behaviours' (Dohnt and Tiggemann, 2006, pp. 141–142).

One Australian study found that among 100 girls aged nine to twelve years, exposure to appearance-focussed media (including *Total Girl*, which is produced specifically for girls aged eight to eleven years, and includes a good deal of celebrity gossip) was indirectly related to body dissatisfaction via conversations about appearance among peers (Clark and Tiggeman, 2007). In other words, 'the more girls talked about topics such as clothes, make-up, and their favourite pop stars, the more they perceived their friends to be focussed upon appearance issues, and the more they themselves internalized these appearance ideals' (Clark and Tiggeman, 2007).

These studies are consistent with a good deal of empirical evidence from studies on adolescent and university-age women (APA TSG, 2007, pp. 23–25).

Apart from disruption to development of a healthy self-image, such body image concerns can be a factor in the development of eating disorders.

Development of eating disorders at younger ages

Amanda Gordon, practising psychologist and president of the Australian Psychological Society, told the Australian Federal government inquiry into the sexualisation of children in the contemporary media: 'I see girls younger and younger becoming depressed. We see girls younger and younger being hospitalised with eating disorders and with concerns about their body and their self-esteem' (SCECA, 2008, section 3.35).

The causes of eating disorders are complex, but experts agree that 'marketing and advertising' contribute to the problem with their 'portrayals of physical perfection' (AMA, 2002, p. 1). Conclusive data is not yet available, but the age at which young people are hospitalised for eating disorders in Australia does appear to be falling,[2] and leading medical professionals have spoken out strongly against the sexualisation of children (Wigg et al., 2006; Wigg et al., 2007).

Severe manifestations of eating disorders have high personal and public health costs. Even 'mild' eating disorders may have side effects on physical health, including headaches, deficiencies in essential vitamins and minerals, bowel dysfunction, tooth decay, dehydration and reduced ability to concentrate and think clearly (CEED, 2008). Such symptoms are likely to have effects on child development more broadly.

Increased self-objectification

Self-objectification is the psychological term for the process occurring when a person emphasises their physical body as seen by others and de-emphasises their own subjective perceptions of themself, such as feeling, knowing, and internal awareness. When a person perceives their own body primarily as an object 'to be looked at and evaluated [for appearance]' rather than perceiving themself as a subject, this is self-objectification (APA TSG, 2007, p. 18).

---

2 Over the period July 2002–June 2005, the Australian Paediatric Surveillance Unit collected baseline data on children (aged five to thirteen years inclusive) with early onset eating disorders. With such baseline data now in hand, over time it will become possible to ascertain more reliably whether young Australians are developing eating disorders at earlier ages.

Self-objectification appears to have a negative impact on girls' performance, both physically and cognitively.

The American Psychological Association Taskforce on the Sexualisation of Girls reported on research in which Anglo and African American girls, aged ten to seventeen years, were asked to throw a softball as hard as they could against a distant gymnasium wall. The researchers found the girls who viewed their bodies as objects and were concerned about their bodies' appearance performed more poorly on the softball throw (2007, p. 22). From this and other research, the Taskforce (APA TSG, 2007, p. 22) concluded that 'self-objectification appears to disrupt physical performance,' and it cautioned that if this leads to girls limiting 'their physical activities, then girls and women are likely to suffer a wide range of consequences for their overall health and well-being.'

The Taskforce (APA TSG, 2007, p. 22) also reported on an experiment that showed that 'self-objectification…fragments consciousness:'

> While alone in a dressing room, college students were asked to try on and evaluate either a swimsuit or a sweater. While they waited for 10 minutes wearing the garment, they completed a math test. The results revealed that young women in swimsuits performed significantly worse on the math problems than did those wearing sweaters. No differences were found for young men. In other words, thinking about the body and comparing it to sexualized cultural ideals disrupted mental capacity.

Healthy and holistic childhood development lays the foundations for healthy and fulfilling adolescent and adult life. The Taskforce (APA TSG, 2007, p. 22) concluded that 'chronic attention to physical appearance leaves fewer cognitive resources available for other mental and physical activities.' This means that the increasing focus on physical appearance in children's lives could impact negatively on their overall development by diverting cognitive resources from other mental and physical activities.

Disruption to healthy psychological development

Professionals working with children believe that sexualised media can confuse children and even disrupt their normal psychological development.

Amanda Gordon (SCECA, 2008, section 3.24) told the Australian Federal government inquiry into the sexualisation of children in the contemporary media:

> [O]ne of the problems [relating to children's understanding of sexualised media] is that many children can understand at a cognitive level, but it is very confusing at an emotional level because they are not yet ready to be sexual, to have those sexual messages.

Jennifer Walsh (SCECA, 2008, section 3.23), education officer at the Australian Research Centre in Sex, Health and Society (ARCSHS), agreed with Gordon:

> We are seeing with primary school children…increasing pressure to present themselves in a sexual way without the mature understanding that goes with that. [More] and more girls [are] feeling that they have to present themselves in a sexually attractive way, finding themselves in situations that they are not mature enough to handle and failing to develop those other aspects of themselves that childhood should allow them to develop normally.

Contribution to increasing child sexual abuse

The sexualisation of children may:

- contribute to creating teenage or adult sexual interest in children where none previously existed; and/or
- lower an important barrier (strong social norms) to child sexual abuse.

47

The American Psychological Association Taskforce on the Sexualisation of Girls (APA TSG, 2007, p. 35) pointed out that the sexualisation of children may contribute to creating teenage or adult sexual interest in children where none previously existed:

> When girls are dressed to resemble adult women… adults may project adult motives as well as an adult level of responsibility and agency on girls…the sexualisation of girls may also contribute to a market for sex with children through the cultivation of new desires and experiences.

The Taskforce (APA TSG, 2007, p. 35) also argued that sexualised images of girls 'may serve to normalize abusive practices such as child abuse, child prostitution, and the sexual trafficking of children.' Bill Glaser, forensic psychiatrist at the University of Melbourne, works rehabilitating convicted sex offenders. Here, he explains how the sexualisation of children undermines his work precisely by normalising the views of child sex offenders:

> [Convicted sex offenders] say, here is all this advertising around the place and surely it cannot be wrong, seeing it is on public display. Some offenders would even use these images almost as a recipe for offending in terms of getting the children or their victims to pose in particular ways (Glaser, 2006).

Some people object to the idea that sexualised images of children could increase the risk of child sexual abuse on the basis that 'stranger danger' from clinically-described paedophiles accounts for a very small proportion of child sexual abuse. The majority of child sexual abuse is perpetrated by people known to the children—often family members. Surely sexualised images of children are irrelevant to these cases of sexual abuse.

About this, Glaser (2005) says:

> The old fashioned idea is that people who offend within the family probably are doing it for reasons other than sexual ones…[M]y own view, for what it's worth, is that people

who offend inside the family often do so because they do have a deviant sexual interest in children, but they stick to the family because that's where their ready-made victims are. That wouldn't of course apply to all offenders inside the family but I suspect that it applies to a great number.

If Glaser is correct, then sexualised images of children, by undermining the strong social norms that prohibit sexual interest in children, may well contribute to the problem of child sexual abuse beyond the small minority of 'stranger danger' cases.

In December 2006, twelve national leaders in children's health, welfare, and media published an open letter in *The Australian* newspaper calling for action to stop the sexualisation of children. They stated clearly that the sexualisation of children leads to sexual risks for children:

> [W]hen commercial forces turn children into sexualised commodities, it corrodes the core of the developing child. These practices set up young children for inappropriate and dangerous roles and behaviours, and make them more vulnerable by far, to sexual danger and harm (Wigg et al., 2006).

Signatories to the letter included senior representatives of: the Australian Childhood Foundation; the Australian Centre for Child Protection (University of South Australia); the Paediatric and Child Health Division of the Royal Australasian College of Physicians; the Centre for Community Child Health, Royal Children's Hospital, Melbourne; the NSW Institute of Psychiatry; and Childwise Australia.

Empirical evidence proving that the sexualisation of children contributes to child sexual abuse may be impossible to obtain. However, many experts are on record arguing that there is a serious risk of the sexualisation of children contributing to child sexual abuse.

We cannot wait for conclusive evidence to act

As just shown, there is a good deal of research evidence and expert opinion that supports the view that premature sexualisation may cause harm to children. In some cases, such as the development of a severe eating disorder or the experience of sexual abuse, premature sexualisation may contribute to irreversible damage to children. For this reason, we cannot wait for conclusive evidence to act. The precautionary principle states that if there is a risk of irreversible harm from an action, that action should not be taken, even if conclusive evidence about the effects of such an action is not available. This principle is often used to argue against environmentally damaging actions, but it can also be used against socially damaging actions.

During the Australian government inquiry into the sexualisation of children in the contemporary media, the vice president of the Australian Council on Children and the Media, Professor Elizabeth Handsley (SCECA, 2008, Section 3.50) used just such an argument:

> [W]e might never know for sure exactly what affects children in what way. But, at the very least, we can say there is some evidence that it is likely that these sorts of images and messages are harmful to children in the long term.

> If we wait until there is absolute 100 per cent proof and nobody can possibly argue anymore that there is no harm to children, the amount of harm that could possibly be done to children in the meantime is immeasurable. So this is a clear example of a situation where a precautionary principle needs to be applied in favour of protecting children from things that are harmful.

3 Responses to critics

People who don't believe the sexualisation of children is a problem tend to use fairly standard arguments. It's handy to recognise these, in order to respond quickly and firmly—whether in the media or at a dinner party.

'There's nothing new about this, children have faced it before and grown up unscathed.'

Wrong. Children have not faced such strong sexualising pressures in the past (see part 1).

'It's simply a matter of taste.'

Wrong. There are risks to children (see part 2). Sometimes discussions can be derailed by differing opinions of precisely where to draw the line between what is appropriate and what is inappropriate for children. Disagreement about the precise categorisation of a particular product (whether it is or is not sexualising) may seem like a matter of taste; whether premature sexualisation in general is a problem is not simply a matter of taste—there are risks to children.

'It's just little girls dressing up and having fun.'

Wrong. There is little creativity (as implied by 'dressing up' in the past) involved, and not necessarily very much fun either, as illustrated by parental reports of eight-year-old girls being teased and ostracised at school for not wearing a bra.

'There is no evidence that children are harmed by sexualisation.'

Wrong (see part 2).

'Child sexual abuse is caused by socio-economic stress, not by cultural messages.'

Child sexual abuse may be more prevalent (or reported more often) in lower socio-economic family situations, but that does not mean that cultural messages are irrelevant. Pinpointing the factors leading to sexual abuse of children is a complex area, and experts in this area, as well as organisations that work with sexually abused children, have spoken out strongly in relation to their concerns about the sexualisation of children (see part 2).

'Parents can prevent premature sexualisation by "just saying no" to their children's requests for sexualised products.'

Parents are very important. They can provide positive role models for their children and talk about the issues with them. However, there are limits to what parents can do without cutting children off from the broader culture. A parent cannot control what occurs outside the home. What is more, to pit individual sets of parents against a hypersexualised culture is unfair. The commercial interests that promote the premature sexualisation of children must adopt more socially responsible practices so that parents, teachers, and other professionals can focus on children's positive development, rather than struggling to undo the damage caused by premature sexualisation.

4 Where to next?

Where commercial interests do not of their own accord move towards more socially responsible practices, the only way to force such movement is to apply public pressure, whether economic or political. With respect to the premature sexualisation of children, consumer boycotts may be effective in specific instances, as might direct action, but the widespread occurrence of sexualising practices and products means these strategies are unlikely to be successful alone. Political lobbying is also necessary, with the aims of obtaining stronger regulation and/or 'shaming' commercial interests into better conduct. The raising of public awareness to support such lobbying is also essential.

References

APA TSG (2007) Report of the American Psychological Association Taskforce on the Sexualization of Girls. Available from: http://www.apa.org/pi/wpo/sexualization.html

AMA (2002) Australian Medical Association Position Statement on Body Image and Health, 2002. Available from: http://www.ama.com.au/web.nsf/doc/SHED-5G4UVU

CEED (2008) Centre of Excellence in Eating Disorders website, 'Health risks of eating disorders' http://www.rch.org.au/ceed/disorders.cfm?doc_id=2832

Clark, Levina and Marika Tiggemann (2006) 'Appearance culture in nine to twelve-year-old girls: Media and peer influences on body dissatisfaction' *Social Development,* 15, pp. 628–643.

Dohnt, Hayley K. and Marika Tiggcmann (2006) 'Body image concerns in young girls: The role of peers and media prior to adolescence' *Journal of Youth and Adolescence,* 35(2), April, pp. 141–151.

Glaser, Bill (2005) Interviewed by *Four Corners* (ABC TV), May 23, 2005, 'Interview—Bill Glaser' (Interviewer: Quentin McDermott). Available from: http://www.abc.net.au/4corners/content/2005/s1375155.htm

Glaser, Bill (2006) Quoted in *The 7.30 Report* (ABC TV), October 11, 2006, 'Institute stands by "Corporate Paedophilia" report' (Reporter: Matt Peacock). Available from: http://www.abc.net.au/7.30/content/2006/s1762698.htm

Rush, Emma and Andrea La Nauze (2006) 'Corporate Paedophilia: Sexualisation of children in Australia.' Discussion Paper 94. The Australia Institute, Canberra. Available from: http://www.tai.org.au

SCECA (2008) Sexualisation of Children in the Contemporary Media. Standing Committee on Environment, Communications and the Arts, The Senate. June. Available from: http://www.aph.gov.au/SENATE/committee/eca_ctte/sexualisation_of_children/index.htm

Wigg, Neil, Joe Tucci, Dorothy Scott, Jane Roberts, Rita Princi, Frank Oberklaid, Louise Newman, Bernadette McMenamin, Patricia Edgar, Freda Briggs, Steve Biddulph, Terry Aulich (2007) Letter, *Sunday Age,* April 16. Available

from: http://www.youngmedia.org.au/whatsnew/
archive_2006-7.htm#apr07_02

Wigg, Neil, Joe Tucci, Dorothy Scott, Jane Roberts, Rita Princi, Frank Oberklaid, Louise Newman, Bernadette McMenamin, Patricia Edgar, Freda Briggs, Steve Biddulph, Terry Aulich (2006) Letter, *The Australian*, December 8. Available from: http://www.youngmedia.org.au/whatsnew/archive_2006-7.htm#dec06_01

The Seduction of Girls:
The Human Cost

Maggie Hamilton

In one Queensland primary school a seven-year-old girl is sexually assaulted over two months by a boy her age. Hitting her and threatening to kill her if she spoke out, the boy repeatedly forced this young girl to perform oral sex (Houghton, 2008, *The Courier Mail*, September 12). In another primary school in New South Wales, teachers struggle to deal with a 'rash' of ten-year-old girls photographing themselves topless, then sending these photos to peers.

Assumptions that girls' lives are the same as those of previous generations leave girls vulnerable—not just teen girls, but tweens and preschoolers. Life has changed radically in a few short years. Young girls are at the cutting edge of these changes. With ready internet access and mobile phones, video and camera-enabled phones, and phones able to download direct from the internet, girls have access to a world of information and experiences. This, along with a steady diet of magazines and sitcoms, movies and music videos, has a huge influence on what girls look and act like, what they aspire to. Most of this material is beyond parental supervision. Some is harmless, much is not.

With these developments has come an explosion in girls' spending, and the ability of manufacturers to access girls direct. The highly competitive tween and teen market, now worth billions, has sparked a proliferation of sexy images and content on billboards, clothing, product wrappers, on screen, in newspapers and magazines, promising girls they can be everything they long to be—attractive, popular, grown-up.

Marketers use sexy images because sex sells. They know that for many girls the combination of sex and shopping is irresistible. The seductive images and language targeted at girls are all the more potent because major companies use a whole range of experts from cultural anthropologists to child psychologists. They know girls' lives intimately and which buttons to press.

'Girls my age want to go out with boys. They think about what they'd like to wear and about shopping,' Vanessa, nine (in Hamilton, 2008, pp. 31–21).

The more sexualised the material we see, the more desensitised to sexual images everyone, including parents, become. Now 'sexy' can refer to anything from a job or apartment, to a partner or pair of shoes. That's why few think to question why products such as Barbie, once only for school-age children, are now available for little girls eighteen months up. Or why little girls are bought slutty Bratz dolls, inappropriately skimpy clothes and tops and accessories with questionable images and slogans.

Girls are big business. Three Barbies are now sold every second (Gregory Thomas, 2007, pp. 134–135). Since the launch of Bratz dolls in 2001, their manufacturer has sold millions of dolls world-wide. As young girls have a very limited life experience, they don't question the sexual imagery and language they see. They naturally assume that's the way things are meant to be.

Decline in imagination

With increasing numbers of young girls addicted to products, pre-school and kindy teachers report a marked decline in imaginative play, and in growing anxieties in little girls around their weight and clothes. In one study of girls aged five to eight, over a quarter of five-year-olds wished they were thinner. This figure rose to 71 per cent for girls aged seven. Most of these young girls felt they had to be slim to be popular. Just under half wanted to be thinner than they were, and were prepared to diet if they put on weight (Womack, 2005, *The Telegraph*, March 8).

These concerns about looks intensify as girls grow. On entertainment TV and in magazines, girls see how much of a celebrity's life and appearance is scrutinised—their hair, boyfriends, children, make-up, skin, weight, clothes, accessories. Aware of this scrutiny, girls begin to take themselves apart. Anxiety is good for business, because it keeps girls purchasing.

Slowing cognitive development

With girls spending more and more time in their bedrooms worrying about how they look and what to wear, they are missing out on the invaluable life experiences needed to develop, and to draw on in difficult situations. Neuroscientist Susan Greenfield is now seeing eleven-year-olds two to three years behind in cognitive development than eleven-year-olds were fifteen years ago. Girls need human interaction, nourishing food and play, and to be directly engaged in life, for their brains to develop. Without these factors, Susan Greenfield believes, their ability to make sense of the world and express themselves creatively will continue to decline (*BBC News*, 2006, September 12).

Plummeting self-esteem

Anxiety and a lack of maturity make girls more vulnerable to marketers and peers. This, and the constant emphasis on how girls look, are major contributors to the concerning growth in self-loathing amongst girls. 'Eight years ago when I did my training as a psychologist, the sexualisation of girls wasn't such an issue. Now girls, even young girls, desperately want to be sexy and beautiful. I'm seeing a lot of young clients struggling with body image and self-esteem,' Gina, a mother and child psychologist told me. 'I see girls at primary school, some in the early years of primary school, worried about looking fat and not being pretty' (Interview with MH, September 3, 2008).

Natasha, a high school teacher, agrees. 'My daughter's only thirteen, but already she takes ages to get ready for school in the morning, doing her hair and everything. She's really picky about what she'll have in her sandwiches. She won't have things like tuna, because she's worried about "tuna breath"' (Interview with MH, September 3, 2008).

As global marketing guru Martin Lindstrom (with Seybold, 2003, p. 196), points out, 'Although this may be the most affluent generation to walk the planet, it also has the dubious distinction of being the most insecure and depressed.'

When life's all about appearance, there's no incentive for girls to value themselves or their unique talents. 'I'm seeing such an increase in troubling situations around girls. Already I'm concerned that the problems we're facing will become more widespread and severe. Girls of twelve and thirteen, who are more artistic and individual, say that while they don't want to conform, they feel they must, to have some chance of surviving at high school,' Gina, a child psychologist informed me (MH Interview, September 3, 2008), adding: 'We need to work with kids to let them know it's okay to be unique, to have your own ideas, as that's how you have a much happier, healthier future.'

Self-harm

As well as a growth in eating issues we see an alarming rise in self-harm. One in ten teen girls is now 'cutting.' Psychologist Lisa Machoian (in Reed, 2007, *The Wellesley*, January 11) goes so far as to describe teen girls self-harming as a 'contagion.' Girls who cut use a whole range of tools from razors and knives, to scissors and glass, or whatever they can find. Girls, some as young as twelve, cut or burn their skin, pull their hair out, or mutilate themselves in other ways to relieve the pain they feel inside.

> I self-injured, starting at around 13, but only causing serious damage much later. Cut myself, burned myself (heat or chemical, either). I will always have the scars. I have stopped, but I still want to, regularly, when I'm sad enough or scared enough, or having trouble coping with how I am doing (Wolfa, February 23, 2005).

Cosmetic surgery

Worried about their looks, an increasing number of girls are turning to cosmetic surgery. Cable reality TV shows such as *The Swan* and *Extreme Makeover* don't help by making cosmetic surgery seem normal, straightforward, risk-free. Here the suggestion is that the best way to deal with body issues is to slice away those parts of the body that don't work, and/or acquire parts that do. Little attention is paid to the pain and discomfort of surgery, let alone the danger that any operation poses or the psychological consequences.

As more celebrities resort to surgery, it doesn't take a huge leap of imagination for teen girls to equate figure enhancement with success. When *Bliss* magazine surveyed girls aged ten to nineteen, more than a quarter of fourteen-year-olds had contemplated plastic surgery (Meikle, *The Guardian*, January 6, 2004). Girls elect surgery in the hope their lives will improve, but as teen cosmetic surgery is relatively new, it's too early to gauge the long-term effects of these procedures. However, one long-term study of over 2,000 women with breast implants is less than encouraging, as these women were found to be three times more vulnerable to suicide in the immediate years following their surgery than those without breast enhancement (Smith, 2004).

Sexualised pre-schoolers

The impact of our sex-saturated culture on girls exposes younger and younger girls to language and behaviours they are not ready to deal with. A growing number of pre-school and kindy teachers report unacceptable sexual behaviour and language from pre-schoolers. They talk of a range of behaviours from tongue-kissing and inappropriate and determined exploration of each other's bodies, to the use of words such as 'sexing' when talking about love and affection. Many parents express similar concerns. One mother of a five-year-old recently told of her daughter's distress at constantly being pressed by a little friend to play 'vagina to vagina.' A day later, the mother of another small girl in a different city was battling this same issue.

'Puberty issues are happening much younger. Some girls are now fashion-conscious as young as three or four,' reflected Debra, a community liaison officer and mother of two girls (MH Interview, September 3, 2008). 'We're now seeing six, seven and eight-year-olds involved in coercive, manipulative sexual behaviours, because there's a confusion around what sexuality means,' said Dr Joe Tucci of the Australian Childhood Foundation. 'This can be very traumatic to the child they're doing this to' (in Hamilton, 2008, p. 53). He went on to explain how the victims often have to undergo intensive counselling to deal with their trauma.

As adults we have been frighteningly slow to realise what is happening to little girls. However, teen girls know intimately the pressures small girls are under, and hate what they see. 'They're like so young and innocent and they should be doing what little kids should be doing, but it's like parents and the media influencing them so much,' Missy, fifteen, told me (in Hamilton, 2008, p. 17).

Girls socialised to be objects

This overwhelming focus on appearances is real and intense, and increasingly is compromising girls' confidence, empathy, and sense of self-worth. The more girls are treated as objects, the more they see themselves this way. When we see teen celebrity and former porn star Jenna Jameson applauded for being 'the single person who's most responsible for bringing porn into the mainstream' (http://www.askmen.com/women/models_250/262_jenna_jameson.html) and hip-hop/rap superstar Snoop Dogg, dubbed as 'America's Most Lovable Pimp,' it's not surprising girls think it's cool to be called a ho or slut (*Rolling Stone*, 2006, November 28).

A growing number of professionals who work with girls are concerned about the objectifying way in which many girls now view themselves. 'What troubles me is that it's like girls don't feel they have any rights,' one high school teacher told me (in Hamilton, 2008, p. 148). 'It's like they want to be objects to be desired.' When I spoke to Poppy, twelve (MH Interview, August 8, 2008), she articulated what many girls now believe. 'You just do all this sex stuff with boys—you don't have to love them or anything.'

When parents are unaware of how girls' lives now differ from their older children's, and from their own experiences, their girls have to find their way through an endless barrage of sexualised images and messages alone. The fallout from this neglect is tangible. 'When I first started teaching in 2000 there was a sense of wanting to be sexy, but it wasn't common for girls to be having sex at twelve—it was more likely at fourteen,' one young teacher told me (in Hamilton, 2008, p. 158). 'Now it's more common at twelve. It's like they want to be wanted and loved in that moment, and that's enough.' Dominque, in *Teen Form* (September 14, 2008) confirms this: '…Okay we have dont [sic] this every day this week…its jus sex no strings attached jus sex after sex, maybe a movie, and more sex.'

With the shrinking of childhood and the collapsing of valuable life experiences, girls are even more vulnerable to doing whatever it takes to be accepted. This same teacher spoke of one student aged fourteen, who took off with a friend in a car full of boys.

During the ride the girl was pressured into taking her top off. She complied because she didn't want to look 'silly.' The boys then took a photo with their mobile and sent it to other kids. When the girl told her teacher, she had no sense of being violated. 'Girls are terrified of being isolated and not being seen as cool,' this teacher explained. 'It was like the girl could only see herself as how boys were seeing her' (in Hamilton, 2008, p. 148).

'There is a huge desensitisation around sexualised images,' agrees one clinical psychologist, who heads up a sexual assault team at a major hospital (MH Interview, September 3, 2008). 'The boundaries have become blurred not just for girls, but their parents, and the whole of society. You can't drive down the street without seeing this material. If these images were put up at work, they'd be seen as sexual harassment, but we constantly see women in pornographic poses on buses and billboards. So, why are we surprised that young girls are participating in rainbow parties and having anal sex? It's been sold to them as empowerment, it's a great con job.'

Performance culture

With ready access to the internet and popular culture, girls are more public about sex, more adventurous about what they'll wear, and what they're prepared to do. Once acts such as oral sex were available only from sex workers. Now they are mainstream. 'For young people it's an almost universal practice now,' says Basil Donovan (AAP, *The Sydney Morning Herald*, 2008, September 16) professor of sexual health at the University of NSW. 'Among teenagers it's the new abstinence in the Clintonesque sense, because it's a way of having sex without having sex, and there are obvious contraceptive advantages too.'

'We're seeing a collapsing of childhood,' warns another psychologist who supports victims of sexual assault. 'Younger and younger children becoming victims of sexual assault. In our performance culture, 'performance' is part and parcel of what's going on with girls.' In their desire to perform for peers, girls are putting themselves in increasingly risky situations. 'Oral and anal sex are now just like kissing. To girls it's not really sex. When their relationship with a boy begins at this level, then the expectations are that they'll be up for a whole lot more' (MH Interview, September 4, 2008).

Teen culture suggests girls need to be primed and ready for sex at all times. And as competition for attention is fierce, the sexual boundaries continue to be pushed. Some girls who are keen to add to their 'repertoire,' access porn for new ideas. Others are getting together with girls, kissing and touching each other, purely to get boys interested. Along with faux lesbianism, teachers talk of a growing interest in threesomes. 'From what the girls say, the boys will think nothing of asking, "Can I have sex with your friend at the same time as well,"' one teacher told me. 'The way things are, it's like it's prudish to say no' (in Hamilton, 2008, p. 145).

Unwittingly, adults have contributed to the burgeoning performance culture. 'Young girls grow up with their lives captured on camera and video by friends and family,' one psychologist pointed out, 'It's only a relatively small step for them or their peers to capture more intimate details of themselves and their life' (MH Interview, September 4, 2008).

'We're seeing a growth in girls being encouraged to take photos of themselves, which can then be used for bribery,' this psychologist explained. 'With threats to tell their parents or new boyfriends what they've been up to, these girls can then be groomed to take more and more explicit photos of themselves. The trauma from these situations can be as bad as physical assault for girls, causing sleeplessness, flashbacks, not wanting to go out—the symptoms of post traumatic stress.'

Sexual assault

While sexual abuse of girls has always existed, according to experts this too is taking new forms. 'We're now seeing girls vulnerable to the same range of risks adult women face—being harmed on their way home by taxi drivers, by boyfriends,' one professional told me (MH Interview, September 3, 2008).

The burgeoning performance culture doesn't help, 'Sexual offenders have less empathy,' this psychologist explained. 'They see their victims as objects. So, the more we encourage girls to view themselves as objects without depth or difference, the more we place them at risk.'

'Personally I have huge concerns. Young girls are now being targeted by older boys,' admits one senior clinical psychologist, who heads a sexual assault support team at a major hospital (MH Interview, September 4, 2008). 'We see a lot of twelve to fourteen-year-olds, targeted by boys seventeen to eighteen years. These are young girls wanting to be grown up, who're still very young and trusting, who fall prey to pre-planned situations. They're plied with alcohol, and possibly drugs, and often raped anally. In the past it was rape by one boy, but now it's two or three boys, and often filmed. The severity of assaults is also growing.' Whitney, eighteen, concurs: 'In some ways it's a bit of a worry porn is what sex is meant to be about. It takes expectations of boys to the extreme. I think that's why rape and sexual abuse is more common now. Porn expresses women in a very different way. I hate the way they like represent themselves like so skankily' (in Hamilton, 2008, p. 147).

The portrayal of girls as objects can have concerning outcomes. One teen actress who appears in a regular TV show, was alarmed recently to discover that the scene of an abduction in which she starred as victim, is now doing the rounds on the internet.

It's no surprise that when talking with many teen girls, they sound as if they're in a war zone. They speak of 'sticking together' and 'watching out for each other,' making sure they're never alone, or their drinks are left unattended. They tell of pretending to drink to look part of 'the scene,' so they won't be made fun of, and of making sure they all leave together.

The very nature, intent and language of marketing is that of seduction. Adults who are marketed to, know this. Girls, particularly young girls, don't. This, along with rapid changes in society, and the explosion of high-tech devices, are having a devastating effect on increasing numbers of girls, because parents and educators haven't caught up.

It's time we stopped focussing on how much money we can make from girls, and look instead at what girls need, to feel confident, to thrive, to be genuinely empowered.

References

AAP (2008) 'Oral sex is on the rise' *The Sydney Morning Herald*, September 16.

BBC News (2006) 'Is modern life ruining childhood?' September 12, http://news.bbc.co.uk/2/hi/uk_news/5338572.stm

Gregory Thomas, Susan (2007) *Buy, Buy Baby: The Devastating Impact of Marketing to O-3s.* Houghton Mifflin, Boston.

Hamilton, Maggie (2008) *What's Happening to Our Girls?* Viking, Penguin. Melbourne, London, New York.

Houghton, Des (2008) 'Sex attack seen as "childhood experiment" at Queensland school' *The Courier Mail*, September 12.

Jameson, Jenna (accessed Sept 2008) 'What We Like About Her.' *AskMen.com*, http://www.askmen.com/women/models_250/262_jenna_jameson.html

Lindstrom, Martin with Seybold, Patricia B. (2003) *BRANDChild: Remarkable Insights into the Minds of Today's Global Kids and Their Relationships with Brands.* Kogan Page, London.

Meikle, James (2004) 'Teen girls just wanna look thin' *The Guardian*, January 6, http://society.guardian.co.uk/publichealth/story/0,,1116982,00.html

Reed, Brad (2007) '"Cutting" on increase in teens, say experts' *The Wellesley Townsman*, January 11, http://www.townonline. com/wellesley/homepage/8999010672477995007)

Rolling Stone (2006) 'America's Most Lovable Pimp,' November 28, http://www.rollingstone.com/news/coverstory/snoop_ dogg_at_home_with_americas_most_lovable_pimp

Smith, Afsun (2004) 'Can bigger breasts buy happiness? No, say scientists: Just the opposite' *Talk Surgery Inc*, May 21, http:// www.talksurgery.com/consumer/new/new00000119_1.html

Teen Form (2008) September 14, http://www.goteenforums. com/forums/peer-yyypyoe-support-a.html

Wolfa (2005) 'I wanna be Angelina Jolie,' February 23, http:// wolfangel.calltherain.net/archives/2005/02/23/i-wanna-be-angelina-jolie/

Womack, Sarah (2005) 'Now girls as young as this five year old think they have to be slim to be popular' *The Telegraph*, Sydney, March 8, http://www.telegraph.co.uk/news/main. jhtml?xml=/news/2005/03/08/nbody08.xml

Sex on the Street: Outdoor Advertising and the Sexual Harassment of Women

Lauren Rosewarne

In preparation for my PhD dissertation and subsequent book, I spent much of 2003 photographing outdoor advertisements. For one year, I photographed every billboard, tram stop advertisement and bus shelter poster that I encountered during my daily commuting. My book, *Sex in Public: Women, Outdoor Advertising and Public Policy* (2007), details the findings of the analysis I conducted on these photographs. For the purposes of this chapter, my central finding was that women tend to be portrayed as young, thin, white and idle. I found that the vast majority of women were in the sixteen to thirty year age category, were in the two slimmest body-shape categories, had white skin and were portrayed doing nothing other than posing. Young, thin, white and idle describes the female characters in outdoor advertising but also describes the women commonly featured in pin-ups. While at the most basic level, the constant display of stereotyped and homogenous representations of women reflects the media sexism that feminists have long bemoaned. Of greater concern, it demonstrates the strong link between advertising images and pin-ups and thus establishes the connection between sexualised outdoor advertising and sexual harassment.

While pin-ups may have artistic merit, their basic function is as a commercial mass-produced image of a woman posing purely for the eye of the (likely male) spectator and to provide that spectator with varying degrees of stimulation. Objectification is the central feminist criticism of media representations: the argument being that including a woman in a media product purely because of her appearance renders her an object and reduces her status to a commodity. Of equal concern is the narrow prescription provided through media images about what constitutes female beauty. While the homogenous young, thin and white aesthetic in advertising presents obvious grounds for criticism, the notion of female idleness raises particular, seldom discussed, concerns.

I embarked on my studies expecting to find images of women engaged in domestic duties, mirroring the way women are routinely portrayed in television advertising. My content analysis, however, refuted this hypothesis: women on billboards aren't vacuuming or tending to children; the outdoor advertising landscape appears largely disconnected from the private world. Interestingly, female central characters have not been relocated to occupational settings either: the public world appears also irrelevant. Instead, the vast majority of women in outdoor advertisements are portrayed against neutral backgrounds and their primary activity is posing, rendering

characters, and their settings, as completely nondescript. Feminist writer Andrea Dworkin discussed pin-ups in a 2000 article, writing that '[pin-up artist Alberto] Vargas' subject—or object, to be more precise—is some lazy, fetishistic view of women, pale women, usually blonde; the drawing itself delineates the boundaries of nonexistence, a white, female nonentity…' (Dworkin, 2000, n.p.). Of critical importance here is Dworkin's idea of women in pin-ups being nonentities. In much outdoor advertising, like the pin -up, the neutral background and the lack of activity presents no information about the identity of the woman: she is simply included to draw attention, rather than lend authority, to the product. Given that many of the advertisements in my data collection reference a woman's sexuality—through revealing clothing, or glossed lips or a parted mouth, for example—her worth is restricted to her beauty and she functions, like the pin-up, as a figure for arousal (see Rosewarne, 2005; Rosewarne, 2007).

The bombardment of images of young, thin, white and idle women highlights many of the concerns feminists have long lamented about the effect of the media on body image, and more broadly, on its connection to sexism, sizeism, ageism and racism. While those are all significant issues, they are also concerns that get extensive airplay in our 'raunch culture' (see Levy, 2005) that is preoccupied with commercialising female sexuality while simultaneously delivering disturbing statistics on everything from prepubescent dieting to obesity. While these

issues are critically important to a discussion of media portrayals, in this chapter, I am more interested in the distraction that such advertising encourages. The homogenous images of women in advertising convey the impression that lifestyle choices like career and family are completely irrelevant: in the world of advertising, the perfect woman is beautiful, decorative and *completely* without identity. For 'real' women, apparently appearance should be their only concern. The woman in advertising exists only as an image to draw attention to a product and as a figure to both establish, and also prescribe, beauty norms. Through her use on billboards purely because of her appearance, the nondescript woman functions to encourage female audiences to aspire to the same aesthetic she reflects. Grave concerns are presented to female audiences who have been coerced into narrow appearance-centered preoccupations. In Lyn Mikel Brown's book *Girlfighting: Betrayal and Rejection Among Girls* (2003) for example, she discusses the consequences of women's narrow focus on image and appearance: 'If we stay preoccupied with our own problems…we won't notice that we are making $0.75 to the male dollar…' (Brown, 2003, p. 32). Brown's comment outlines a clear—and disturbing—consequence of allowing our focus to centre on micro-issues such as individual appearance: equality struggles fall by the wayside.

It has been over forty years since US feminist Betty Friedan exposed the problem of sexism in advertising in her book *The*

Feminine Mystique (1963)
and yet the advertising landscape today boasts levels of
objectification and sexualisation Friedan likely could
never have imagined. One
notable development is
the incorporation of refer-
ences to pornography. Just
as pin-ups have gotten pro-
gressively more explicit, so
too have outdoor advertisements. Four examples from
my data collection highlight
this well. In a Coca-Cola
advertisement, a bikini-clad
woman has her lips around
the top of a Coke bottle, the
text 'You know you want it'

is printed across the top. A *Harper's Bazaar* advertisement showed a
woman in a mini-skirt, her head tilted back, her right hand pushed
down the front of her singlet, cupping her breast. A billboard for
the Moonee Valley Races displayed a woman with a riding crop,
the caption reading 'Experiment at Night.' A billboard for the
BMG record label showed the pop singer Pink wearing a low-cut
leather swimsuit, restrained by ropes. These four advertisements
draw on our knowledge of pornography and in turn reference
fellatio, masturbation, sadomasochism and bondage and discipline,
and use these allusions to sell soft drinks, magazines, a gambling
venue and CDs. Given there has been over forty years of feminist
awareness about sexist imagery and yet the problem today is worse,
we need to move beyond thinking about this issue as purely one
of sexism. For the problem to be treated as serious and as something requiring urgent action, we need to consider the issue as a
serious public policy problem. Public space is a public good and

thus the images displayed in it need to be appropriate for the entire audience who is not only exposed, but held captive, to these public images. Sexual harassment in the workplace encroaches on the rights of individuals and can inflict a variety of negative consequences, notably making victims feel excluded from their workplace or their place of study. A very similar situation occurs in public space where women can feel excluded from public space through continual exposure to images that may embarrass, offend or otherwise harass. While feminist awareness and activism on this issue has had limited success, I propose that approaching this issue as a public policy concern and offering actual solutions to this problem are key to changing the advertising landscape.

I address the shortcomings of current advertising control in *Sex in Public* (2007) and propose a series of policy solutions. For individuals concerned by the content of advertising, the time to quietly lament is over. In 2002, the Victorian Office of Women's Policy in Australia published a report titled 'The Portrayal of Women in Outdoor Advertising.' An interesting section of this report focussed on participation in the complaints procedure. The report detailed that of the 37 per cent of female respondents who had seen an inappropriate outdoor advertisement, only four per cent formally complained. Of the male respondents, 32 per cent thought about complaining, but no man actually did. When asked why formal

complaints were not made, 22 per cent of respondents claimed that
they did not know who to complain to, thirteen per cent thought
no-one would listen, and ten per cent did not know how (OWP,
2002, p. 13). In most western countries, advertising is 'controlled'
through self-regulation: in Australia this is done by the Advertising
Standards Board. The outdoor advertising landscape looks the way
it does for many reasons, an obvious explanation being that people
simply do not formally articulate their complaints and their silence
is read as tacit approval, or at the very least, as acceptance. People
offended by outdoor advertising need to contact the Advertising
Standards Board and formally submit a complaint. Through making that complaint, the Board—as well as the advertiser who is then
contacted by the Board—is made aware of your offence. Yes, it is
highly likely that the Board will reject the complaint—it is after
all, a board assembled by the industry working *for* the industry to
protect the industry from the 'heavy hand' of government—but by
formally complaining, the grievance is put on the record, which
helps to deliver to advertisers a true gauge of public sentiments
(see Gale, this volume). Currently, community silence on sexism in
advertising is read by advertisers as agreement, if not *encouragement*,
and thus the landscape remains a gallery of highly sexualised images
of women that harass and exclude.

The stereotyped images of women in outdoor advertising highlight a troubling public policy double standard whereby images
that are completely prohibited in a workplace or school, are somehow okay for public display. It is *not* okay. The inescapable, unavoidable features of outdoor advertising that make the medium
so tantalising to advertisers, are the same elements which make
public space a public good and necessitate that the displays within
are suitable for the *entire* audience held captive: women as well
as men and children. Audiences cannot restrict their exposure to
outdoor advertisements; therefore contents need to be restricted
to avoid socially excluding, offending and sexually harassing those
held captive to them.

All photos were taken by the author.

References

Brown, Lyn Mikel (2003) *Girlfighting: Betrayal and Rejection Among Girls*. New York University Press, New York.

Dworkin, Andrea (2000) 'Vargas' Blonde Sambos' *No Status Quo*. Retrieved July 7, 2008, from http://www.nostatusquo.com/ACLU/dworkin/vargas.html

Friedan, Betty (1963) *The Feminine Mystique*. Dell, New York.

Levy, Ariel (2005) *Female Chauvinist Pigs: Women and the Rise of Raunch Culture*. Free Press, New York.

OWP (February, 2002) *The Portrayal of Women in Outdoor Advertising*, July 8, 2008, from http://www.women.vic.gov.au/web12/rwpgslib.nsf/GraphicFiles/Outdoor+Advertising+Report/$file/outdoor-advertising-report.pdf

Rosewarne, Lauren (2005) 'The Men's Gallery. Outdoor advertising and public space: gender, fear and feminism' *Women's Studies International Forum*, 28 (1), pp. 65-76.

Rosewarne, Lauren (2007) *Sex in Public: Women, Outdoor Advertising and Public Policy*. Cambridge Scholar's Press, Newcastle, UK.

The Psychological and Developmental Impact of Sexualisation on Children

Louise Newman

Introduction

Rosa (pseudonym) is an eight-year-old girl living with her parents and ten-year-old brother. Like many girls her age she is interested in music videos and fashion. She reads magazines aimed at the 'tween market' and collects images of older girls she would prefer to look like. She copies dance moves and styles she sees on television and wants to wear similar clothes. For Rosa this interest has become preoccupying. She has become anxious and told her mother that she is not good looking enough to be popular at school. She says she is fat and starts restricting her diet in an attempt to lose weight. She is depressed and tearful. She says she will never have a boyfriend. Her school work is neglected and she is referred to the school counsellor and to a child mental health service.

Jane (pseudonym) is a fifteen-year-old girl being treated for depression and low self-esteem by a mental health service. She is a reserved young woman and is intelligent but underperforming. She has little motivation to succeed at school and struggles to see herself as having control over her own life. She feels unattractive and says that she has few qualities that will help her fit in socially.

She has low self-esteem and has become isolated. Jane judges herself against media representation of female attractiveness. She sees sexual activity as a way of gaining popularity and has entered into poorly judged and exploitative relationships with older boys. She feels abandoned and rejected. Jane is confused about what she should expect in relationships and thinks that having sex will lead to closer emotional relationships.

The 'sexualisation' of children refers to the imposition of adult sexual themes and images on children at a developmentally inappropriate stage and in a way which may compromise child psychological development. It includes overt sexual imagery as well as the reinforcement of adult definitions of attractiveness for children and young people. In the extreme it involves the use of children for adult sexual gratification and child pornography. This has aroused significant public concern and calls for increased regulation and monitoring of the exposure of children to adult sexual themes. With sexualised images seemingly proliferating, we need to ask if we are damaging children by exposing them to sexual themes either directly or indirectly.

In many ways this is a deceptively simple question and one that has prompted a heated debate. Polarised views are expressed with some denying the existence of so-called 'sexualised' images of children, let alone evidence that these may put children at developmental risk. The debate as it has unfolded has tended to be reduced to one about the rights to sexual expression and discussion. Those who have raised concerns about the use of adult sexual themes and images in overt marketing to children, or in a way that exposes children to adult material, are labelled as puritanically 'anti-sex.' Those in favour of sexual themes in community spaces are (self-styled) as libertarian, anti-censorship and paradoxically pro-feminist. Somewhere in the midst of this are real issues concerning the needs of children for care and protection from exploitation, and the rights of children and adolescents to sexual development and expression as developmentally appropriate. The parameters of the debate are not always clear, with little attempt to define what 'sexualisation' of children refers to and the difficult issues around clearly defining sexual exploitation and measuring the longer term impacts of 'premature' sexual exposure.

Despite these inherent difficulties, this is without doubt a matter of concern for child protection and mental health groups and one where models of child development are central. Various child developmentalists and child advocates are urging greater regulation of this material in the interests of children, but even this is contested by the 'freedom of expression' argument. The 'sexualisation' debate could be better informed if based on understanding contemporary models of children's social and psychosexual development and the impact of sexual trauma on psychological health. There is a clear need to separate the child protection issues from the rights of adults to sexual expression and community values around this.

Several key issues arise in this debate. Have attitudes towards public use of sexual themes changed in western societies and for what reasons? Are more children exposed to adult sexual themes and images and is this necessarily resulting in psychological harm? Are there long-term consequences of any sexual exposure? Are there particular values promoted in sexualised material? The central issues then are around exposure, content, implicit values and consequences.

Child sexual development

Sigmund Freud (1905/1976) created great controversy by describing the sexual nature of infants and children and the key role of sexual feelings in human development. By breaking a major taboo he paved the way for thinking about the role of parenting and the importance of children's early experiences in shaping later sexual functioning and relationships. For Freud, children were 'sexual' beings, but 'infantile' or childhood sexuality was not equivalent to adult sexuality. The young child is learning about sexuality in the context of relationships with parents and has a series of developmental stages prior to reaching any defined adult type sexual identity involving sexual preference and the capacity to enter into relationships involving sexuality and emotional intimacy. Freud described the child's development of sexual identity as closely related to the development of ideas of gender identity and generational roles. An excess of sexual arousal, or conversely, excess anxiety around sexual expression, may result in difficulties in sexual development. As far back as 1896, Freud was concerned that repression of sexuality or early sexual trauma could result in developmental problems.

Many of Freud's early ideas about sexual development remain important. Whilst current terminology may be different, the concept of childhood sexuality and the understanding that children are interested in, and experience, bodies and sexual feelings and have emergent models of sexuality, are central to most developmental accounts. The parent or adult carer of the child shapes the child's experience of their body and designates some bodily parts as 'sexual,' but at the same time does not engage with the child as a sexual partner or object. The adult understands the child's experiences as 'child-like' and does not see them as adult sexual behaviours. If the adult cannot maintain the separateness and distinction between adult and child sexuality, the child is exposed to confusing and disturbing anxieties.

Exposure of children to adult sexual images may be confusing and disturbing for young children who have not yet come to understand the nature of sexual interactions. Involving children directly in adult-type sexual imagery such as having them wear adult style fashion and underwear and engage in 'mimicry' of adult sexual behaviours is likely to be more disturbing. It fundamentally denies the existence of the child's need for their own sexual development and the difference between adult and child sexuality. Both are developmentally inappropriate and ignore the difference between child and adult sexuality.

Child sexual exploitation

The World Health Organization Consultation on Child Abuse Prevention (2006) defines child abuse as the following:

> Child abuse or maltreatment constitutes all forms of physical and/or emotional ill-treatment, sexual abuse, neglect or negligent treatment or commercial or other exploitation, resulting in actual or potential harm to the child's health, survival, development, or dignity, in the context of a relationship or responsibility, trust or power.

The prevalence of child sexual abuse or use of children for adult sexual gratification varies according to definitions and sources of information. As the WHO 2006 report finds from international studies conducted since 1980, mean lifetime prevalence rates are twenty per cent among women and five to ten per cent among men. In most countries girls are at higher risk than boys for sexual abuse, neglect and forced prostitution.

This is a broad definition and encompasses practices such as the use of images and depictions of children for adult sexual purposes or commercial gain and direct sexual exploitation as in abuse and trafficking. WHO estimates that 150 million girls and 73 million boys under eighteen experienced forced sexual intercourse or other forms of sexual violence during 2002 (2006, p. 63). Recent estimates indicate that in 2000, around 1.8 million children were involved in prostitution and pornography and 1.2 million were victims of trafficking (UNICEF, 2007).

In the context of increasing reports of child abuse and exploitation, increasing use and access to child pornography and greater understanding of the damaging impact of child abuse on development and mental health, the concerns about child exposure to sexual themes are serious. Arguments about what constitutes 'sexualised' images are perhaps distracting given the reality of child abuse, and may be seen as an attempt to stifle debate about cultural trends towards greater sexual exposure and the values inherent in this. It is important to analyse cultural representations of gender roles, sexuality and relationships and ask what specific values are being promoted and if these are having a negative impact on child development. Key questions include the impact on children of a phenomenon described as 'raunch culture' and celebrity images; the impact on girls of stereotyped images of passivity and sexual objectification; and the long-term impacts of early exposure to adult sexual themes and the ways in which cultural exposure impacts on parents' roles in protecting and educating children around sexuality in a developmentally appropriate way.

Sex sells: child exposure to sexual images

Children are both primary and secondary targets of sexualised images used in commercial marketing. The direct marketing of adult type 'sexy' clothes to children is one example of conscious manipulation of fashion trends for commercial gain. The secondary exposure of children to adult sexual themes in advertising, text and images is also of concern in that it presents children with information and relational themes they may not understand and which may arouse premature questioning. Whilst adults can elect to discuss or ignore some of this material, children are potentially influenced by the array of material and are less able to 'filter' this by selective attention. Children learn by observation and imitation and are influenced by the 'packaging' of material by things such as music, dance and colour. They respond to the cumulative amount of exposure and the inherent values and communications. Advertising (print, outdoor and television), girls' magazines and free-to-air television, increasingly present an array of adult sexual themes as well as material aimed at children (particularly girls) around sexual attractiveness, sexual images and fashion, all reinforcing a particular female self-image and identity.

Research

The American Psychological Association's 2007 review of the proliferation of sexualised images of girls and young women in the media concluded that there is a clear impact on girls' self-image and development. Sexualisation was defined by the APA Taskforce as a process whereby the individual's self-worth or value is defined in relation to sexual appeal or behaviour or, if the person is sexually objectified and used for another person's sexual purposes. For girls in particular the implicit message in these types of representations is that female identity revolves around sexual attractiveness to men and that a girl's value as a human being is measured in these terms. Opposing values, such as self-determination, self-confidence and assertiveness and positive images of autonomous female roles are either not represented or again 'turned into' an image thought to be sexually attractive to men by suggesting that strong females are 'sexy.' Of particular concern are the use of representations of pre-pubertal and young girls as 'sexy' with an inherent message that even young girls need to be socialised as early as possible into the defined female role.

The research evidence reviewed by the APA (2007) finds that girls and young women are negatively impacted by sexualised images in several ways:

1 Cognitive and emotional development—sexualised images are associated with girls developing anxiety, low self-esteem and body-image concerns;
2 Mental health problems—sexualisation is associated with the development of disordered eating behaviour, depression and low self-esteem;
3 Sexual development—sexualised images present a negative role for girls and women in sexual relationships and damage the development of healthy sexual self-image.

Of particular concern is the way in which sexualisation impacts on self-development. Girls exposed to sexualised images and representations of girls and women as sexual objects internalise these images and values and can incorporate them as part of their self-identity. This results in self-scrutiny, anxiety about appearance, self-consciousness and low self-esteem. Unrealistic media representations of female bodies and a 'beauty ideal' contribute to body dissatisfaction in girls and concerns about weight and appearance. Increasing numbers of adolescent girls seek plastic surgery and cosmetic procedures such as botox injections.

Frequent exposure to such culturally specific beauty ideals has produced a commercially significant market in beauty products, diet and weight loss products and programs and appearance preoccupation, even in primary school age children. Children are also exposed to adult sexual themes and preoccupations in the forms of advertising, radio and television items and general exposure to erotic print material and clothing in general stores. Whilst this is not specifically aimed at children or young people it unavoidably influences children's perceptions and social learning regarding sexuality and relationships. Again, the marketing of a 'raunch' culture or set of attitudes concerning sex and gender may have far-reaching impact on children's development. Further research will be important here. We need to see the development of new strategies for children to understand and evaluate the complex messages delivered in the contemporary media.

Challenges for mental health services and child protection

Mental health and support services for children and young people are well aware of the impact of advertising, media and gender stereotypes on development. Like parents, they often feel overwhelmed in the face of the degree of exposure that children experience, and the difficulties vulnerable children and young people have in disengaging themselves from distorted representations of sex and relationships. Teaching media literacy and strategies for resisting distorted representations is a powerful strategy: to be effective it should be introduced in primary school. A more complex issue is that of child risk in the face of the proliferation of sexualised child images. Recent controversy around the depiction of pubertal girls in art (see Bray, this volume), and ongoing concerns about very young models in adult style fashion representations are seen by some as the minority views of those in favour of censorship. Such labelling is not conducive to a sophisticated discussion about the needs to protect children from abuse. While it may only be a minority who will read these images as directly 'sexual' in the sense of finding them erotic and being motivated to act on this, the consequences are significant.

In the midst of the debate about advertising of children's clothes, I received a phone call from an anonymous person describing his use of this advertising material for sexual pleasure. He described his confusion that his particular paedophilic sexuality was condemned on the one hand, but for him, reinforced in media and advertising in an explicit way on the other. He concluded that this proved that sexual use of children for adult purposes was legitimated by this message. He did not see that his sexual attraction to children was in fact disordered or damaging and that he was drawn to images reflecting his interests in the media and advertising. Like many paedophiles, he denied that the involvement of children in adult sexual behaviour is damaging and in fact argued that children were interested in sexual relationships with adults and might even benefit from this. This rationalisation of harm to children is a key feature of child sexual offenders and is known to be resistant to change. It poses a significant risk of ongoing abusive behaviour as the offender justifies their behaviour to themselves and shows little regard for the victim.

How can we best protect children, but at the same time promote open and healthy learning around bodies, sexuality and gender? The broader issues of representation of girls and women in harmful and demeaning ways has been long challenged but continues to

83

operate and perhaps in a more insidious fashion as it is now linked to an image of sexual 'freedom' and autonomy. Children who are developing their understanding of sexuality and sexual roles are not in a position to unpack the complexity of cultural messages delivered by the media and advertising. As in the two examples described at the beginning, girls especially may be made anxious and vulnerable in the face of a seemingly monolithic and sustained pressure to conform. Restrictions on advertising to children and scrutiny of the sorts of representations children are exposed to are not censorship, but a process of child protection that takes account of the developmental vulnerabilities of children and their unique developmental pathways—and helps children like my patients Rosa and Jane.

References

American Psychological Association (APA) (2007) 'Taskforce on the Sexualization of Girls.' Report retrieved from www.apa.org/pi/apa/sexualization.html

Finkelhor, David (1999) 'The international epidemiology of child sexual abuse' *Child Abuse & Neglect*, 18 pp. 909–17.

Fonagy, Peter (2006) 'Psychosexuality and psychoanalysis: an overview' in Fonagy, Krause and Leuzinger-Bohleber (Eds) *Identity, Gender and Sexuality: 150 Years After Freud*. IPA Press, London. pp. 1–21.

Freud, Sigmund (1905/1976) *Three Essays on the Theory of Sexuality*. Standard Edition 7. Penguin, London.

UNICEF (2007) 'Reference guide on protecting the rights of child victims of trafficking in Europe.' Retrieved from www.unicef.org/publications

World Health Organization (2006) 'Global estimates of health consequences due to violence against children.' Background paper for the UN Study on Violence against Children. www.who.org/publications

Good Is the New Bad: Rethinking Sexual Freedom

Clive Hamilton

The ethic of consent

It is now evident that the removal of most taboos and social prohibitions on sexual activity has led to a highly sexualised society in which erotic imagery and sex talk are to be found everywhere in both private and public life. This has been the enduring influence of the sexual revolution of the 1960s, which saw the replacement of traditional moral prohibitions with the 'ethic of consent.' According to the ethic of consent, when third parties are not affected, informed consent is the only ground for judging the moral value of behaviour. In these situations, there is no 'morality,' only an agreed procedure for individuals to decide 'what is right for them.'

This form of individualism is the ethical basis of both free market libertarianism and the social demands of the sexual revolution. So unlimited sexual expression has become bound up with notions of freedom to the point where, for many people, it provides the path they follow in order to find and validate themselves.

It seems to me that this state of affairs could come about only because the idea of sexual relations has been unconsciously but essentially redefined. After contraception had virtually eliminated biological reproduction as a factor in sexual decision-making, especially for men, there seemed to be only one function left—the pursuit of pleasure. Yet, as explained in my book *The Freedom Paradox* (2008), there is a third aspect of sexual engagement that goes beyond its physical pleasures and the biology of reproduction. It concerns the idea of union, both emotional union and what might be called metaphysical union, the direct expression and joining of our inner selves, our essence as humans.

The evocation through sexual union of some mysterious power that holds the promise of ecstatic merger gives sex a significance that transcends everyday experience. I think the power of this little-discussed but ever-present aspect of sexual engagement, in which contact between bodies can take us beyond physicality, explains our society's preoccupation with sex in all of its manifestations.

Casual sex

Casual sex, if freely consented to, is engaged in purely for physical gratification and perhaps for the emotional pleasure of a brief social encounter. Sex without love is widely practised among younger adults in western countries, and few are willing to criticise it. If both parties freely agree and are over the age of consent, what possible objection could there be?

Before attempting to answer this question, we need to think about the context in which casual sex has proliferated, since in practice it is a minefield of potential consensual ambiguities. In the first instance, each party must be old enough, sober enough and sane enough to be able to take moral responsibility for their decisions. In practice, we know that youthfulness, drunkenness and emotional distress among women are exploited by men to sexual advantage.

And it is not only girls whose emotional confusion can be exploited. The newspapers report cases of schoolboys aged fourteen or fifteen who are invited or seduced by their female teachers into sexual relationships. The typical reaction of men reading about these cases is to wish they had been so lucky at school, yet this popular flippancy is contradicted by the fact that few of the seduced boys escape without emotional trauma, sometimes severe and long-lasting.

There is also a wider set of pressures on people, especially young people, to engage in casual sex. The market is saturated with sexualised imagery and content whose effect is to create and reinforce the view that engaging in sex is a natural part of social life and that those who do not participate will be ostracised. The 'cool' group at high school acquires its elevated status primarily by engaging in, or giving the impression of engaging in, sexual activity. Sex is associated with sophistication, non-conformity and a willingness to embrace life.

Perhaps the most disturbing aspect of the pervasiveness of sex is advertisers' practice of presenting children in sexually provocative clothing and poses to sell products, a marketing method sometimes referred to as 'corporate paedophilia' (see Rush, this volume). This is done by even the most respectable companies. The coexistence of widespread alarm about paedophilia and society's apparent indifference to children being presented in the media as sexually desirable stands as a striking testimony to the power of denial on a mass scale.

Where both parties truly consent to a casual encounter, and no third parties are affected, making moral judgements is a mistake. However, a friend or family member might assume the role of moral adviser. The friend of a young woman considering a sexual encounter might question whether the proposed liaison is really in the young woman's interests. Is consent freely given or is the young woman feeling pressured? If she gets drunk will she be in a position to consent? Is the sex engaged in for its own sake or is there another objective? Although the scene is presented here as an interrogation, young people engage in these sorts of conversations almost daily, often taking advice from magazines.

If the young woman can answer honestly that none of those factors presents an obstacle and all the conditions of fully informed consent apply, her friend might pose a final question. Will you regret it afterwards? In posing this question, the friend is calling into the conversation the young woman's moral self, her inner judge.

Why might the young woman regret engaging in casual sex even though she goes into the encounter fully informed and consenting? One view, put by ethicist John Hunter (1980), argues that impersonal sex always falls short of 'sex with love.' The latter goes far beyond physical gratification: it includes 'mutual trust, total mutual acceptance, and an intimacy distinguished by the sharing of one's innermost thoughts as well as one's body.' Sex in the context of love and intimacy becomes part of a rich relationship marked by security and reciprocity, which nurtures the sense of value and specialness in the lovers that infuses their entire relationship and advances their health and emotional wellbeing.

Hunter's argument is that casual sex does not live up to an ideal, but for our young woman the choice is not between casual sex and ideal sex: it is between casual sex and no sex. A contrary view, in support of impersonal sex, is described by Raymond Belliotti (1993) who argues that people who pursue sex without love might be seeking only the inherent pleasure of sex and value a life free of emotional entanglements. Impersonal sex may be more enjoyable, he says, because it is free of oppressive expectations and obligations.

This is a point of view widely expressed, especially by younger people. Yet feelings of regret often follow casual sexual encounters. If, after the event, the young woman's inner judge rules against her, the disturbance she feels—apart from disappointed physical and emotional expectations—will be for something she has relinquished, a gift that has been spurned. The metaphysical intimacy of joining essences she and her partner experienced, has no emotional context and so might feel like a violation of her bodily integrity and a trivialisation of sexual union. For both men and women, if emotional intimacy is absent, metaphysical intimacy feels hollow, for its special character seems to require care and respect.

Perhaps this is why many people are left with a vague feeling that each time they have casual sex they give away a little of themselves, that something sacred is profaned, and they are diminished as a result. Casual sex truly becomes meaningless sex.

In an era when premarital sex attracts no stigma and, indeed, self-restraint must be defended, this seems to be at the heart of the decision by some young women, and even some young men, to go against the trend of sexual licence and 'save themselves' for their partner in a long-term committed relationship.

The return of self-restraint

For teenage girls in the 1950s the price of breaching the chastity rule could be high, especially if they became pregnant. By the 1970s, virginity had become a sign of oppression, a denial of the right to free sexual expression. But 30 years on, sexual self-restraint is making a comeback. Recently, one young woman, now twenty, said that when her school friends became sexually active at about fifteen, depression, confusion and rejection often went with it (Overington, 2008). In a sex-saturated culture her peers felt they had no choice. 'They were blind in a way,' she said, 'doing what they thought they had to do with their boyfriends. They should have been told they didn't have to behave that way.' But the only message from the adult world was 'Use a condom.'

This young woman made a bold decision—to abstain from sex until she feels the time and the person are right. Her friends saw it as a bit weird but also fascinating. So perhaps the wheel is turning. Where once teenage sexual activity was a sign of rebellion, now girls and boys who say 'no' have become the dissenters. This refusal signals independence of mind. I am not, of course, talking about campaigns or ceremonies that pressure young people to make commitments to abstain; I am talking about young women, and men, who make a considered choice and decide on the basis of their own free will.

Once only the timid and compliant held back from sex; now it is the confident and courageous who refrain. Which leads us to wonder: who is more free—the young woman for whom sex is too valuable to be given over to the culture of the one-night stand, or her friends who became sexually active at fifteen because it is expected of them?

Who's in control?

The objective of the social revolutions of the 1960s was to replace a society of oppressive rules and conventions with a society of autonomous individuals committed to the welfare of all and discriminating against none. For the first time we would be free to control our own destinies. Yet today we have never experienced more pressure to define ourselves in ways determined by others, including the marketing industry.

For decades, psychologists have collected data on a personality trait called the 'locus of control,' a measure of the extent to which we believe we control our own lives rather than being subject to outside forces. The research, by psychologist Jean Twenge (2004) shows that since the 1960s, young people in the west have become *more* inclined to believe external forces control their lives. Remarkably, declining scores on locus of control tests are greater among young women, despite the opportunities for women delivered by the feminist movement. Perhaps we should expect no more of an era in which for many the socially acceptable life is the one lived out of control—binge drinking, indiscriminate sex and capitulation to every desire. 'Equality' has come to mean freeing girls to behave as badly as boys and creating a new gender, 'girls with balls,' where once we imagined perhaps something closer to boys with ovaries. Contrary to the arguments of some 'pro-sex' feminists, when young women mimic the boorish behaviour of young men, it is still men who set the standard. Raunch culture debases the dream of liberation.

The demand for individual rights in the 1960s released a self-centredness that has grown into full-blown narcissism. In the pursuit of tolerant pluralism a society of rampant individualism was created, a phenomenon dubbed 'boomeritis' by author Ken Wilber (2006). Appeals to the principles of equality and freedom often allowed egocentric demands to flourish. Slogans such as 'Let it all hang out' and 'Do your own thing' were soon interpreted as 'No one can tell me what to do.' Self-worth became self-worship.

The marketing language used today mirrors this development precisely. Narcissistic interpretations of liberation are the bread and butter of modern advertising. Consider these tag lines from magazine ads: 'Go on, you deserve it.' 'Just for you.' 'If it makes you happy, it's a bargain.' 'I don't care what it is, I want it.' It is now apparent that the demands of the liberation movements dovetailed perfectly with the logic of hyper-consumerism. The self-creating individual was the agent ideally suited to the needs of the market. Among the first to understand the opportunities this presented were the tobacco companies, which turned 'women's lib' into dollars by associating smoking with women's emancipation and empowerment. As early as 1968, Phillip Morris launched Virginia Slims, a cigarette brand targeted specifically at women, famously deploying the slogan 'You've come a long way, baby.'

The strategy worked: more teenage girls took up smoking. A magazine ad in 1978 juxtaposed a photo of an elegant woman in an evening gown with one of a housewife hanging out the washing. The text read, 'Back then, every man gave his wife at least one day a week out of the house. You've come a long way, baby. Virginia Slims—Slimmer than the fat cigarettes men smoke.' Sadly, the tumours women developed were no slimmer.

We cannot be free if we become slaves to our passions. But is not the absence of inner freedom the dominant characteristic of modern consumer society, where the cultivation of momentary impulse, temporary emotions and moral and intellectual weakness has become the essence of the system? Is not the purpose of the marketing society to make us slaves of our passions? In the era of hyper-consumerism the urge to satisfy any desire has reached sublime levels. It is now possible to buy capsules filled with 24–carat gold leaf which, when swallowed, make your excrement sparkle. Created by New York designer Tobias Wong, the gold pills are promoted as a signifier of excess and a means of 'increasing your self-worth'—although presumably for only as long as the digestion process takes. At $425 each, they are the ultimate confirmation of the ancient association, often noted by anthropologists, between gold and excrement.

This is the freedom of the market. Rosa Luxemburg once wrote: 'Freedom is always and exclusively freedom for the one who thinks differently' (1920, p. 109). She was right; thinking for ourselves is the ultimate form of liberty. Yet who truly thinks differently today when our universities have become locked in to the demands of the market, corporations infiltrate the academy and governments drain funds from the critical disciplines? Who thinks differently when the mass media saturate the culture with triviality and when children's brains develop in a vat of commercial messages?

Where is the space for different thinking when 'the end of politics' has been announced, where a particular form of liberal capitalism has achieved such hegemony that there is no substantive difference between the main political parties because they have converged on a belief in unfettered markets, consumer choice and the primacy of economic growth?

Bad girls

The narcissistic and self-destructive elements of boomeritis converge in the figure of Paris Hilton. In September 2008, Republican presidential contender John McCain ran a television ad subliminally associating Barack Obama with the emptiness of Hilton's celebrity; like Hilton, suggested the ad, Obama is the creation of pop culture. The Republican's strategy failed because, in conspicuous contrast to the previous Democrat president and unlike Paris Hilton, Obama represents the antithesis of pop attitudes to sex.

Barack and Michelle Obama's public kisses and embraces have turned them into the 'hot couple' who are making sex in marriage look not only desirable but better than the alternative (Wypijewski, 2008). In the old mind-frame of the 1960s, sizzling matrimonial love seems an oxymoron, but the Obamas are making it 'cool' to be monogamous. For young people who have chosen sexual autonomy, perhaps even abstinence, the Obamas seem to provide a model of how intimacy and commitment can be combined with a great sex life.

Post-modern academics see the 'bad girl' as the heroine who sticks two fingers up at the puritanical repression of healthy sexuality (Lumby, 1997). But against Michelle Obama, the bad girl looks more and more like the puppet of a hypersexualised society whose demands to conform are every bit as insistent as those of the 1950s conservatives. She is a victim of the teen culture satirised in films like *Mean Girls* and in Chris Lilley's character Ja'mie in *Summer Heights High*. All Ja'mie wants is to be 'hot.'

'Bad' no longer signifies rebellion but compliance. Withholding the body instead of flaunting it—acknowledging one's sexuality but not necessarily sharing it with strangers—is the new 'transgression.' Good is the new bad.

The reappearance of sexual self-restraint does not, however, represent a return to the conservative morality of the 1950s, with all its oppressive baggage. The argument for sexual self-determination is an argument for *more* freedom, not less—freedom from the tyranny of expectations imposed on baby boomers' children by the commercial co-option of the aspirations of the sexual revolution. The task for today's teenagers is to win back their freedom from the adults who run the advertising agencies and girls magazines and the 'sex-positive' media academics who insist that 'bad girls' are powerful girls.

The idea of empowerment through sexual licence has reached its pinnacle in the case of Natalie Dylan, a 22-year-old Californian who is auctioning her virginity to the highest bidder. 'I understand some people may condemn me,' she said. 'But I think this is empowering. I am using what I have to better myself' (Anon, 2008). In a perfect convergence of the narcissistic interpretation of 1960s sexual liberation and pure market thinking, she declared: 'I don't have a moral dilemma with it. We live in a capitalist society. Why shouldn't I be allowed to capitalise on my virginity?' Why not indeed? If he requests it, the purchaser of Natalie's virginity will be able to authenticate the quality of the product by way of a gynaecological examination and then consummate the transaction in a brothel. Nice. As if to underscore the perversion of the ideals of feminism, it turns out that Natalie holds a bachelor's degree in women's studies.

Post-modern sex radicals who urge teenage girls to seize power by being sexually provocative are the new oppressors, because they insist that teenagers behave according to their own 1960s script. The same people defend the liberating possibilities of pornography, which is supposedly liberating for women because it breaks through the regulation of women's bodies to show, in the words of one, 'the disordered side of the female body—its orifices and fluids—which are both threatening and exciting' (quoted in Lumby, 1997, p. 76). So efforts to regulate porn are always 'the puritanical repression of healthy sexuality' (quoted in Lumby, 1997, p. 77).

On this view, criticism of any form of sexual behaviour is suspect because all sexuality is deemed natural and because the suppression of one form of sexual expression can only be the thin end of the wedge. This gives rise to some grotesque arguments. Thus one defender of 'bad girls' could in all seriousness declare on national television in Australia (and in print) that those who want to regulate advertising to control the premature sexualisation of girls are equivalent to the Taliban who want to cover girls in burkas and make them the property of men (Fine, 2007).

The debate over the sexualisation of girls has outed these post-modern libertarians. They have always argued that children are sexual creatures and should be allowed to explore and express their sexuality without the guilt imposed on them by neurotic adults and conservative clerics. Children are much smarter than neurotic adults, they believe, and can slip easily into a savvy, ironic, critical mode whenever there is any danger of falling under the sway of advertisers or media.

The politics of this are bizarre, for there has emerged an unholy alliance, or concordance of interests, between certain post-modern academics and the most aggressive agents of consumerism, the marketing industry (including the porn industry). Both argue that advertising has no untoward influence on consumers, including child consumers, but is merely informational and entertaining. Thus the post-moderns, who matured in an era of challenging the powerful and denouncing oppressive structures, have ended up as their most loyal apologists.

Rebuilding

The sexual revolution failed to deliver on its promise of a world of uninhibited sexual pleasure for all, in which we could find and express our true desires. Sexual freedom was never equal and became burdened with expectations it could never meet. Pursuing sexual freedom as an antidote to boredom or as a means of finding personal fulfilment was always a doomed adventure, particularly as it continued to reflect a male-centred idea of sex. For many—first men but increasingly women and now girls—it became a means of avoiding emotional intimacy and shunning the metaphysical meaning of sexual union. The ideology of sexual freedom did not recognise that, for all of its wonders, sex also has a powerful dark side, one that often gives rise to feelings of betrayal, regret and emptiness.

I have argued that engaging in early and uninhibited sex was once a sign of rebellion against an oppressive orthodoxy; now in a sex-soaked society, in which the imagery and practices of pornography are seeping into the mainstream, a new orthodoxy has taken hold, imposing a set of expectations almost as oppressive as those it replaced. In this new environment, power is now to be exercised by resisting those pressures so that deciding to abstain from sex can be an expression of self-control, of inner freedom. Today the challenge is no longer to attack and tear down, but to rebuild a moral code that truly liberates and leads to fulfilled lives for both women and men.

References

Anon (2008) 'Shock jock to auction off girl's virginity: Howard Stern announces his most controversial stunt yet' *Daily Mail,* September 9.

Belliotti, Raymond (1993) *Good Sex: Perspectives on Sexual Ethics.* University of Kansas Press, Lawrence.

Fine, Duncan (2007) 'Paris is good for kids: Sexed up, dumbed down, Hilton evokes an escape from the Western Taliban' *The Australian,* May 18.

Hamilton, Clive (2008) *The Freedom Paradox.* Allen & Unwin, Sydney.

Hunter, John (1980) *Thinking About Sex and Love.* Macmillan, New York.

Lumby, Catharine (1997) *Bad Girls.* Allen & Unwin, Sydney.

Luxemburg, Rosa (1920/1983) *Die russische Revolution. Eine kritische Würdigung,* Gesammelte Werke Band 4. Dietz Verlag, Berlin (Ost) 1983.

Overington, Caroline (2008) 'Abstinence makes the heart grow fonder for real love, not sex' *The Australian,* July 14.

Twenge, Jean, Liqing Zhang, and Charles Im, (2004) 'It's beyond my control: A cross-temporal meta-analysis of increasing externality in locus of control, 1960–2002' *Personality and Social Psychology Review*, 8 (3), pp. 308–319.

Wilber, Ken (2006) *Integral Spirituality*. Integral Books, Boston.

Wypijewski, JoAnn (2008) 'Obama as sex symbol' *The Nation*, August 4, 2008.

The *Faking It* Project: What Research Tells Us about Magazines in Young Women's Lives

Selena Ewing

What's your body for? What's it supposed to look like? Is it for other people to look at and use? Who's telling *you* what it should look like, and what it should be doing?

For millions of young women all over the world, these questions are answered by glossy fashion and lifestyle magazines. They have been around for decades. These days, such magazines are mostly written and produced by women, for women.

We recognised the significance of this media form in women's lives. The burning question for Women's Forum Australia[1] was this: are these magazines beneficial and empowering for women and girls? To answer this question, we took the academic, evidence-based approach that informs all our work. We scoured peer-reviewed journals for research about magazines, pop culture, body image, and women's health.

---

1 Women's Forum Australia is an independent women's think tank involved in research, education and advocacy on issues affecting the wellbeing and freedom of women.

What we found was far too important to remain locked away in journals or academic reviews where few young women would ever read them. A crucial requirement of the project was to make our report something people wanted to read. And so *Faking It*, an evidence-based parody of glossy women's magazines, was born.

We produced *Faking It* because we believe young women should know what they're really getting when they pick up a women's or girls' magazine. They should be able to read about, if they want to, what researchers and psychologists have found out about how media images portray women and how they affect women. They should also know that how thin, beautiful and sexy they are is *not* a measure of their value. And that they don't exist solely to be looked at and judged, or to be sexual objects for men.

As soon as we began to promote our project, we realised that there are large numbers of people in and outside Australia who are deeply concerned about magazines, about media messages, and about the avalanche of images of 'perfect' sexualised women that we face in everyday life. Until recently, they have been a silent majority. Why silent? Partly because the objectification of women has become normalised through a hypersexualised pop culture. That is to say, we live in a world saturated in images of artificial, perfect, semi-naked, 'sexy' women in all manner of unreal positions and environments. It's not easy to go against the grain. It's not easy to challenge something that is presented to us as empowering, modern and mainstream.

Many people have told us that they feel unable to explain their concerns. They feel embarrassed, prudish or old-fashioned to speak up.

There are two things that we want to tell those people. Firstly the weight of scientific evidence is on their side. There *is* something to be worried about. The research in *Faking It* shows that media portrayals of women as sex objects is bad for girls' and women's health. It's not about censorship, or taking the high moral ground; it's about women's wellbeing.

There are academics and researchers thinking and writing who have the language and the evidence to support their concerns. We want to make these tools available to people who otherwise might remain silent.

Secondly, it has become clear that there are vast numbers of people supporting what we're doing. We have held successful *Get Real* events in eight cities around Australia, with thousands of women attending, and have received overwhelmingly positive feedback and appreciation. Grassroots movements can have great power in changing things, even changing cultural trends. What we've been seeing over recent months is a groundswell of public opinion against premature sexualisation, and against sexual objectification. This is a movement of concerned parents, educators and health activists and, importantly, it is supported by the strength of research evidence.

Our research in *Faking It* is an important tool in this movement. The findings are sometimes shocking and often illuminating, helping to make sense of the media onslaught to which we are subjected every day. Many girls and women have directly responded to us: 'So I'm not the only teenager who detests her own body?' 'What is it about fashion and beauty advertisements that somehow make me feel fat and ugly?' 'Why do I feel depressed after reading a girls' or women's magazine that I chose to purchase and read?'

After reviewing reams of research from peer-reviewed academic journals, we're not convinced that glossy mags are empowering for women. Many other researchers are worried too. Most of them are psychologists and others come from the disciplines of health, economics, feminism, politics, and language. *Faking It* draws together a variety of approaches into one resource that demystifies the impact of women's magazines on women's lives.

It would not be fair to say that all glossy women's magazines are the same. In some ways they are all a little different, yet in many key ways they're very similar. There seems to be a winning formula that sells the most copies—notice, for example, how all the covers are very much the same. It's not just the cover graphics and layout, but the phrases on the cover. The themes and the philosophies seem to be very similar—perhaps even predictable.

The headlines are always a combination of fashion, beauty, men and sex. Advertisements in these magazines, as well, combine to send a clear message to the person checking out the cover in the supermarket. What is this message? It is this: to be happy and normal, young women should be thin, sexy and beautiful. They should spend much time and money achieving that look. And here are the women they should look like—celebrities, supermodels, and porn stars, sometimes young women who do nothing but dress up and party hard—the new role models for today's young women.

In addition, young women should have a man and they should be having lots of hot sex with him. Because everyone else is. At least, that seems to be the message from your average magazine.

The idea that your body, how you look, and especially your sexual parts, *are* your whole self is known as objectification. It is an idea that comes at the expense of recognising that women are complex, whole and intrinsically valuable individuals with intellectual, emotional, physical, and spiritual capacities, and that we have unique talents and interests. It makes empty shells of us.

When pop culture repeats over and over, in images and messages, that women are most valued for their looks and their bodies, women might begin to believe it. Enter the very scary phenomenon called self-objectification. Young women who believe this idea will be devoting most of their energies towards meeting ideals of physical perfection—which, by the way, are based on digitally altered images of carefully selected women, and therefore completely unattainable.

Self-objectification involves the over-valuation of shape and appearance, and research shows that self-objectification and perfectionism can result in women submitting their bodies to constant surveillance, comparing themselves to media images, and ending up feeling intensely ashamed of their own bodies (Tiggemann and Kuring, 2004; Tylka and Hill, 2004; Hebl, King and Lin, 2004; Evans, 2003; Durkin and Paxton, 2002; Pinhas, 1999; Thornton and Maurice, 1997; Monro and Huon, 2005). It affects women's everyday activities, with some studies showing that self-objectification can result in compromised intellectual and motor performance (Fredrickson et al., 1998; Fredrickson and Harrison, 2005; Gapinski, 2003; Strelan, Mehaffey and Tiggemann, 2003; Segar, Spruijt-Metz and Nolen-Hoeksema, 2006; Tiggemann and Williamson, 2000).

Researchers have analysed magazines in a few different ways.

One way is to come up with some classifications for all the pictures, including advertisements. They make codes for what the people in the pictures are doing, what they're wearing, how they're posed, and so on. Then they do statistical analyses of the pictures and their meanings. Using this method, some researchers (Krassas, Blauwkamp and Wesselink, 1997) concluded that the US edition of *Cosmopolitan* sent a very similar message to the one of the US editions of *Playboy*—that women have an insatiable appetite for sex, and must be continually available to men. And both magazines mainly had pictures of women—very few pictures of men. *Cosmopolitan* is the most widely-read women's magazine in many countries, including Australia.

If this is indeed a message that *Cosmo* and perhaps other magazines are sending, this presents at least two problems for young women.

Firstly, research shows that we are influenced in our sexual behaviour—even against our better judgment—by what we think everyone else thinks, and by believing media messages that suggest everyone else is doing it. Teenagers in particular want to fit in and be accepted. And as research shows, and people intuitively know, media messages are very powerful. Why else would anyone bother advertising? Advertising is a billion-dollar global industry and those who claim that young people can just ignore advertising are naïve.[2]

Secondly, because sex is often portrayed as young women's main currency, many young women feel they have to make excuses for why they don't want sex. Not wanting sex is so unusual, according to pop culture, that it's either a personal insult to the man in question, or it's evidence that the young woman is prudish or dysfunctional in some way.

Young women also tend to highly value their relationships, and be eager to please others, so saying no to sexual advances can be very difficult. Not to mention the fact that young women who are ashamed of their bodies or who have very low self-esteem are particularly vulnerable to sexual advances, sometimes seeing even the worst of them as flattering (Brumberg, 1997).

Another way of analysing magazines is to try to understand the messages in the articles. British researchers (Machin and Van Leeuwen, 2003) were interested in the advice given to women in the UK edition of *Cosmopolitan*. Their research identified a theme, a philosophy, in the advice to women. It was 'it's up to *you* to take action to solve your own problems.'

Some people might see this as an empowering message to women; but how empowering is it really to suggest that your problems are all your own, and that no-one else needs to be involved in solving them? This is a lonely, false message, and, above all, it is the message of an individualist consumer culture.

The reality is that women are, and need to be, part of communities and families. And most of our problems aren't simply private, individual matters. There are in fact social, economic, structural, historical and many other reasons why women are faced with particular problems, especially in terms of relationships and sexual encounters. Women's Forum Australia looks especially to public

2   For an expose of how advertising affects us, read Jean Kilbourne's book *Can't Buy My Love: How Advertising Changes the Way We Think and Feel* (1999).

policy, education and advocacy to help women be their best. We are very wary of those who expect women to change themselves while everyone and everything else remains the same. We are especially concerned with those who believe women should just buy a product, or pop a pill, or undergo a procedure, to solve their alleged problems like low self-esteem, or being apparently different to others, or failing to have those hot sexual relationships that popular culture expects everyone to have.

So some messages might be false or a little fanciful. Does it really matter what we read and look at? Isn't it just a bit of entertainment?

Unfortunately not. Another research direction that you can read about in *Faking It* is an analysis of how women think and feel before and after reading magazines. Their reactions might be observed in the short term, or over a period of years. Researchers have looked at women's beliefs about themselves, their bodies, about other women, their eating and exercise behaviours, and other aspects of their lives, in relation to the media to which they are exposed.

One very clear finding is that there are harmful effects of being exposed to pictures of thin and glamourous women. Poor body image, lower self-esteem, anger, anxiety, shame, self-surveillance are documented responses (Groesz, Levine and Murnen, 2002; Pinhas et al., 1999; Evans, 2003; Durkin and Paxton, 2002; Thornton and Maurice, 1997; Monro and Huon, 2005). Put differently, research shows clearly that what we see really does affect us. This is serious stuff. Women may not realise this is happening to them; they may not make any connection between the glossy, beautiful, popular magazines and the negative, often hidden aspects of their own lives. Sometimes research and advocacy are necessary to cast light on these connections.

Fortunately, occasionally positive things happen that we can applaud. The Australian edition of *Cosmopolitan* has made at least two good moves recently. One is to ban diets. The other is their Body Love Policy that ensures differently-sized women are pictured throughout the magazine.

We think it is also positive that *Girlfriend* and other magazines sometimes write about accepting yourself as you are, and sometimes make a point of admiring those who are considered larger-sized models and celebrities rather than just young women who look like stick insects (a particular feature in *Faking It*). In fact since publishing *Faking It* we have noticed many women's magazines featuring articles on body image, finding celebrities who are willing to discuss more frankly their own body image issues, and to show their bodies in a more realistic light.

Nevertheless, in spite of these good things, the expectation to look good and to be sexy remains a priority in these magazines. And on balance, the messages dominating these magazines, especially as a result of the advertisements, effectively drown out any efforts of well-meaning editors and journalists to provide positive, realistic messages.

After all, page after page of sexy, perfect models in advertisements do not correspond with a message that you're okay the way you are, or that your intellectual achievements matter as much as how 'hot' you look, or that you don't need a man to be a fulfilled woman.

It's a paradox: if the editors really want to empower women, their ambition is scuttled by the fact that the very existence of these magazines is tied to advertising. In most advertising aimed at women's fashion and beauty products, women need to be made to feel like they're not good enough in order to spend their money on the product in question.

Faking It has struck a chord with thousands of women and girls, proving to be a very effective way of unlocking the research about how magazines speak to us and impact upon our lives. Sometimes the mass media needs to be drawn back to reality, to be accountable for the damage they may be doing. And sometimes the wider community needs to be given a nudge to act, and a voice to speak. Our aim is to do all of that, and to help girls and women to resist the pressure to fake it, and to keep it real.

References

Brumberg J.J. (1997) *The Body Project: An Intimate History of American Girls.* Random House, New York.

Durkin S.J. and Paxton S.J. (2002) 'Predictors of vulnerability to reduced body image satisfaction and psychological wellbeing in response to exposure to idealized female media images in adolescent girls' *Journal of Psychosomatic Research* 53, pp. 995–1005.

Evans P.C. (2003) '"If only I were thin like her, maybe I could be happy like her": the self-implications of associating a thin female ideal with life success' *Psychology of Women Quarterly* 27 pp. 209–214.

Fredrickson B.L., Roberts T.A., Noll S.M., Quinn D.M. and Twenge J.M. (1998) 'That swimsuit becomes you: sex differences in self-objectification, restrained eating, and math performance' *Journal of Personality and Social Psychology* 75 (1), pp. 269–284.

Fredrickson B.L. and Harrison K. (2005) 'Throwing like a girl: self-objectification predicts adolescent girls' motor performance' *Journal of Sport and Social Issues* February 29 (1), pp. 79–101.

Gapinski K.D. (2003) 'Body objectification and "fat talk": effects on emotion, motivation and cognitive performance' *Sex Roles: A Journal of Research* 48 (9/10), pp. 377–388.

Groesz L.M., Levine M.P. and Murnen S.K. (2002) 'The effect of experimental presentation of thin media images on body satisfaction: a meta-analytic review' *International Journal of Eating Disorders* 31 pp. 1–16.

Hebl M.R., King E.B. and Lin J. (2004) 'The swimsuit becomes us all: Ethnicity, gender, and vulnerability to self-objectification' *Personality and Social Psychology Bulletin* 30 (10), pp. 1322–1331.

Kilbourne, Jean (1999) *Can't Buy My Love: How Advertising Changes the Way We Think and Feel.* Touchstone Rockefeller Centre, New York.

Krassas N.R., Blauwkamp J.M. and Wesselink P. (2001) 'Boxing Helena and corseting Eunice: sexual rhetoric in *Cosmopolitan* and *Playboy* magazines' *Sex Roles* 44 (11/12), pp. 751–771.

Machin D. and van Leeuwen T. (2003) 'Global schemas and local discourses in *Cosmopolitan*' *Journal of Sociolinguistics* 7 (4), pp. 493–512.

Monro F. and Huon G. (2005) 'Media-portrayed idealised images, body shame, and appearance anxiety' *International Journal of Eating Disorders* 38, pp. 85–90.

Pinhas L., Toner B.B., Ali A., Garfinkel P.E., Stuckless N. (1999) 'The effects of the ideal of female beauty on mood and body satisfaction' *International Journal of Eating Disorders* 25, pp. 223–226.

Segar M., Spruijt-Metz D. and Nolen-Hoeksema S. (2006) 'Go Figure? Body-shape motivations are associated with decreased physical activity among midlife women' *Sex Roles* February 54 (3/4), pp. 175–187.

Strelan P., Mehaffey S.F. and Tiggemann M. (2003) 'Self-objectification and esteem in young women: the mediating role of reasons for exercise' *Sex Roles* 48 (1/2), pp. 89–95.

Thornton B. and Maurice J. (1997) 'Physique contrast effect: adverse impacts of idealized body images for women' *Sex Roles* 37 (5/6), pp. 433–439.

Tiggemann M. and Kuring J. (2004) 'The role of body objectification in disordered eating and depressed mood' *British Journal of Clinical Psychology* 43, pp. 299–311.

Tiggemann M. and Williamson S. (2000) 'The effect of exercise on body satisfaction and self-esteem as a function of gender and age' *Sex Roles* 43 (1/2), pp. 119–127.

Tylka T.L. and Hill M.S. (2004) 'Objectification theory as it relates to disordered eating among college women' *Sex Roles* 51 (11/12), pp. 719–730.

The Gaze that Dare Not Speak Its Name: Bill Henson and Child Sexual Abuse Moral Panics[1]

Abigail Bray

Pulease, pulease leave me alone…For Christ's sake leave me alone.

Vladimir Nabokov, *Lolita* (1958, p. 194)

The lesson of photography is that there are many truths, not one…People do sometimes only see what they want to…The greatness of art comes from the ambiguities, which is another way of saying it stops us from knowing what to think. It redeems us from a world of moralism and opinionation and claptrap. It stops us in our tracks as we are formulating the truths we think we believe in. It stops us and makes us wonder.

Bill Henson (in Shanahan, 2008)[2]

What is the lesson of Henson's photographs of naked girls? How did the Australian 2008 'moral panic' over Henson's photographs of a naked thirteen-year-old girl bring to the surface hidden

---

1   This chapter draws on Bray, 2009, 'Governing the gaze: child sexual abuse moral panics and the post-feminist blind spot.'
2   For the full text of the Henson speech see http://fddp.theage.com.au/pdf/Bill%20Henson%20speech%NGA.pdf

cultural rules about who can and cannot see the commercial sexual exploitation of children? How do we situate a gaze that '*redeems us from a world of moralism and opinionation and claptrap?*' (my emphasis) Whose world and whose gaze is being humiliated and silenced here as mere moralism, opinion and claptrap?

'After a regrettable period of moral panic', reported *The Australian* on June 7, 2008, 'the Bill Henson affair appears to have been resolved in an appropriate and welcome manner' (cited in Marr from *The Australian*, 2008, p. 131). From an edgy beginning in sociology text books of the 1970s to an upwardly mobile term that radiates cultural capital, 'moral panic'—and especially 'child sexual abuse moral panic'—has become code for the intolerant tabloid emotions of the moralising masses, rampaging menopausal vigilantes in council states, vulgar man–hating feminists, the mindless authority of the state, bleating Christians and sundry 'holier–than–thou–f*cktards.'[3] One simply does not suffer from 'vulgar' child sexual abuse moral panics when one is a sophisticated, socially progressive and responsible, neoliberal, middle-class subject.

In brief, the 'regrettable period' in question followed a complaint about a photograph of a naked thirteen–year–old girl on the invitation to Henson's private opening at the elite Roslyn Oxley9 Gallery in Sydney. For several weeks after the police temporarily confiscated Henson's photographs on May 22, 2008, on the grounds that they might represent child pornography, the Australian mass media was involved in a debate about censorship, art and child pornography. Immediately after the new Labor Prime Minister Kevin Rudd commented that Henson's photographs were 'absolutely revolting,' members of the Australian Creative Taskforce reprimanded Rudd in a petition, warning him that the Henson child sexual abuse moral panic would create 'untold damage to our cultural reputation.'[4] As Henson's lawyer flippantly put

---

3   The phrase 'holier–than–thou–f*cktards' is from the blog http://fearofemeralds. livejournal.com/6261.html and the section called 'You bastards—Bill Henson and the paedophilic gaze.'
4   See David Marr (2008) for an uncritical discussion of this event. See also Mathew Westwood and Corrie Perkin (2008) 'Artists jump to Henson's defence.'

it: 'The subtext of my opinion was, don't be the laughing stock of the world' (in Marr, 2008, p. 121). Indeed, numerous media articles, opinion pieces in major newspapers, Australian and British blogs declared that a child pornography censorship moral panic was threatening the very foundations of Australian democracy. Celebrating an aesthetic appreciation of Henson's shadowy photographs of limp, melancholic naked girls with hairless vaginal folds and budding breasts became a way of being seen as a cool, rational, cosmopolitan Australian.

'They're *very* beautiful, they're *very*, *very* still, they're *very* formal, they're *very* classical. They're a bit like looking [sic] an ancient Greek Attic vase,' commented Judy Annear in a *Sydney Morning Herald* article on May 23, 2008. And while 'his images may take the viewer to an edge, to an uncomfortable place…it's like great music or great literature. I don't look at Henson's work and see it as anything other than a broad field of possibilities' (in Grattan, 2008). Australia's leading cultural left journal *The Monthly* commented that: '[A]rt, at its best, often makes us feel uncomfortable. Many of us long for this discomfort, because we feel it opens onto truth' (Smee, 2008, p. 62). Ironically, however, an *uncomfortable* feeling by Henson critics that the photographs were celebrating a heterosexual, paedophilic sexual aesthetic was outlawed as nothing more than a vulgar child sexual abuse moral panic.

Henson eventually triumphed—the charges were dropped after a couple of months—but in the meantime cultural critics had transformed the event into further proof that child pornography censorship legislation is limiting freedom with increasingly oppressive systems of surveillance and control. As Anna Munster (2009, p. 6) opines:

> Although charges against Henson were not pressed, artistic image making will become increasingly monitored by police and concerned citizens alike and the climate for artistic ambiguity, the pursuit of difficult topics and the distribution of images will narrow.

Indeed, according to a range of experts across the disciplines, child pornography censorship legislation is one of the more nefarious symptoms of the child sexual abuse moral panics which emerged from the PC politics of 1970s feminism. In this context, not only is child pornography censorship legislation responsible for persecuting the innocent 'brilliance' of internationally acclaimed artists such as Henson, this '[d]isproportionate reaction to an exaggerated menace' (West, 2000, p. 528) causes childhood obesity and mental illness, vigilantes and tabloid legislation, the debasing of all relationships between adults and children, the social construction of children's sexuality and the eroticisation of innocence. As the Henson 'affair' demonstrated, the perception by critics that his photographs were sexualising children, was *pathologised* as a symptom of a dangerous child sexual abuse moral panic disorder.

However, as Mieke Bal (1993, p. 400) writes '[t]here are many ways of looking around; only we don't see them because there are certain gazes that take all the authority.' To such a critical gaze, Henson's nocturnal photographs of thin, shy, fragile girls, his deliberate manipulation of shadow in order to draw attention to their budding breasts and hairless vaginal folds, belong to a context which goes beyond the genteel walls of upper-class art galleries and the in-bred world of art critics. This context is as unruly and uncomfortable as a streetwise recognition that while growing up, a girl too often learns the humiliating heteronormative rules of sexual inferiority from men who do not even bother to conceal their paedophilic intent and who know only too well that a child's voice poses no threat to a culture that is governed by the voices of adult male authority. This 'impolite' context is populated by the whispered confessions of girls, shared warnings, fears, the countless stories of women about their childhoods, being stroked and pushed, about screams, pain, self-disgust, shame, wanting to die, wanting to break free. The girl in one of Henson's photos reminds me of the shocking impact of sexual objectification on a child's body. Her withdrawn, melancholic naked body reminds me of the paralysis of shame, of the humiliating interest of adult men who mask their intrusions as sexual compliments that demand gratitude not anger, obedience not rebellion. She reminds me of the discourse of Lolita, of the sexual politics of 'jailbait,' of films such as Louis Malle's *Pretty Baby* (1978), or Sonny Boy Williamson's 1937 'Good Morning Little School Girl,' of the incessant nudge and wink of a culture which plays with the 'rift between decency, male interest and the profit margin' (Rush, 1980, p. 126), of the sexual deregulation of the market place, and the global triumph of a paedophilic sexual economy. Her meek silence and downcast eyes remind me of how difficult it is to speak back to something which one is forbidden to.

Several months after the Henson affair one of his photographs was quietly auctioned in Australia for $3,800 by Menzies Art Brands. Lot 214, the black and white 'Untitled 1985/86' (see Henson, 2009) peers down on a naked child on the crumpled sheets of a bed, her knees bent, her legs wide open, her face turned away from the camera, her lips parted, her expression blank. She is wearing childish bangles on both arms and an ankle 'slave' bangle. Her hair is in a ponytail. Her vagina and budding breasts are highlighted by Henson's trademark manipulation of shadow. The girl is anonymous. However, to see the ugly sexual political context of Henson's photographs is to be dismissed as hysteric, prude or worse.

As Anne Higonnet (1998, p. 153) argues:

> The sexualisation of childhood is not a fringe phenomenon inflicted by perverts on a protesting society, but a fundamental change furthered by legitimate industries and millions of satisfied consumers (also in its minor way by the art world).

However, the very phrase 'sexualisation of childhood' risks minimising a radical shift in the sexual politics of girlhood: what still remains largely unspeakable is the possibility that this historically recent change is about mainstreaming the old self-serving masculinist fantasy that girls are 'up for it' Lolitas. As the Bill Henson episode shows us, this very suggestion is currently being mocked as an unsophisticated moral panic. The irony is that in the name of anti-censorship, we are forbidden to name the new sexual politics of childhood. The Bill Henson episode suggests that this unofficial form of censorship is preventing important dialogues about the patterns of inequality that are being produced by the commercial exploitation of children's sexuality. In 1980, Florence Rush (pp. 191–192) wrote that:

> The concept of sexual liberation as the last frontier in the struggle for freedom closed the 1960s with *The Sensuous Woman*. The concept of children's sexual liberation has closed the 1970s with *The Sensuous Child*. When sexual liberation becomes synonymous with political revolution a movie such as *Pretty Baby* can pass as a radical intelligent work of art and the new avant-garde can advise that "Every child has the right to loving relationships including sexual, with a parent, sibling, other responsible adult or child"…Today's idea of sexual liberation and the sexual freedom of children is a euphemism for sexual exploitation, and at the rate we are going, today's sexual freedom may well become tomorrow's "opiate of the masses."[5]

The cultural shift Rush identified almost three decades ago has, arguably, become normal to the point of invisibility. Challenging the sexualisation of girls is not the same as policing, pathologising or denying their agency. The problem is that their agency is read as sexual. They do have agency, they think, make choices, but this is not the same as adult agency. It is the relentless *sexualisation of girls' agency*, and not agency itself, which is the problem. The sexualisation of girls' agency just becomes another way of mystifying sexism when all that girls are free to do is participate in burlesque versions of older sexual stereotypes. Being sexier or having more sex doesn't magically do away with sexism. It is surely naïve to argue that within this brave new masculinist world of compulsory sexual self-empowerment girls 'kick ass.'

---

5   The quotation is from Valida Davila, 'A Child's Sexual Bill of Rights,' Sexual Freedom League Childhood Sexuality Circle, cited in Rush (1980, p. 192).

As Rosalind Gill points out in 'Empowerment/Sexism: Figuring Female Sexual Agency in Contemporary Advertising' (2008) '[T]he figure of the "unattractive" woman who seeks a sexual partner remains one of the most vilified in popular culture...'The unattractive, desperate, needy loser circulates as a cruel warning to girls about the dangers of not being sexy enough. The monotonously transgressive sexualisation of girls and women carries new forms of sexual humiliation: to be sexy or not to be sexy is no longer the question—one must be sexy if one is to escape social humiliation. Just as 'victim' has become a code word for a failure to take responsibility for one's choices, the new culture of sexual humiliation is disguised as nothing more than a girl's failure to 'kick ass.'

In an era in which challenging the commercial sexualisation of girls has become equated with a disempowering denial of children's agency, the responsibility of adult agency and adult corporations is frequently airbrushed out of the all too glamorous picture. Just as it has become cool to argue that girls are no longer innocent victims but rather self-empowered sexual agents, artists such as Henson have become the innocent victims of child sexual abuse moral panics. To put it another way, in the name of sexual liberation the bodies of children have been emptied of 'innocence' while artists such as Henson have instead become the new innocents, strangely passive, vulnerable and in need of protection, the new victims of moral panics about children.

We need to unmask the political 'innocence' of artists such as Henson, and more broadly, of a culture that trades in the sexual commodification and humiliation of girls. Far from offering girls new forms of social power, the sexualisation of girls' agency is imposing a new tyranny of compulsive and desperate sexual participation.

It is vital that we continue to ask whose gaze and whose history is being silenced by the *panic* about child sexual abuse moral panics. If prohibitions are now circulating which are preventing a critical engagement with the sexual politics of the corporate and artistic sexualisation of children, then surely it is vital that we shake off this cruel and blind neoliberal indifference and begin to worry about why we no longer dare to speak out. Perhaps, in the end, the lesson of Bill Henson's photographs is that it is vital that new thinking about the sexualisation of children interrupts this cool indifference and opens up cultural spaces in which we have the courage to see differently.

References

Bal, Micke (1993) 'His master's eye' in D. Levin (Ed) *Modernity and Hegemony of Vision*. University of California Press, Berkeley. pp. 370–404.

Bray, Abigail (2009) 'Governing the gaze: child sexual abuse moral panics and the post-feminist blind spot' *Feminist Media Studies*, 9 (2), pp. 173–191.

Fearofemeralds (2008) 'Bill Henson and the paedophilic gaze' May 25, http://fearofemeralds.livejournal.com/6261.html

Gill, Rosalind (2008) 'Empowerment/Sexism: Figuring Female Sexual Agency in Contemporary Advertising' *Feminism & Psychology* 18; 35 http://fap.sagepub.com/cgi/reprint/18/1/35

Grattan, Michelle (2008) 'Is the art fuss justified?' *Sydney Morning Herald*, May 25, http://www.smh.com.au/news/opinion/michelle-grattan/is-the-art-fuss-justified-2008/05/24/1211183174659.html

Henson, Bill (2009) 'Untitled 1985/86' at http://www.menziesartbrands.com.cgi?file=DM=15772.jpg&text=&width=400 accessed 23 June, 2009.

Higonnet, Anne (1998) *Pictures of Innocence: The History and Crises of Ideal Childhood*. Thames and Hudson, London.

Marr, David (2008) *The Henson Case*. Text Publishing, Melbourne.

Munster, Anna (2009) 'The Henson photographs and the

"network" condition' *Continuum,* 32 (1), pp. 3–12.

Nabokov, Vladimir (1958) *Lolita.* Putman, New York.

Phillip, Richard (2008) 'Australia: Labor Government Backs Witch-hunting of Photographer Bill Henson' *World Socialist Web,* May 26, http://www.wsw.org/articles/2008/may 2008/raidsm26-prn.shtml

Rush, Florence (1980) *The Best Kept Secret: Sexual Abuse of Children.* McGraw-Hill, New York.

Shanahan, Leo (2008) 'After the outrage' *The Age,* July 11, http://www.theage.com.au/national/after-the-outrage-henson-steps-out-among-friends–to-defend-art-and-artists-20080710-3d6p.htm

Smee, Sebastian (2008) 'Unsettled' *The Monthly: Australian Politics, Society and Culture,* November, pp. 60–62.

Sydney Morning Herald (2008) 'Henson a "whipping boy"' May 23, http://www.smh.com.au/news/arts/henson-a-whippingboy.2008/05/23/12118306044/8.html

The Australian (2008) 'A good outcome' June 7, http://www.theaustralian.news.com.au/story/0,,23823316-16382,60.html

Wells, Hal M. (1978) *The Sensuous Child.* Stein and Day, New York.

West, D. (2000) 'Pedophilia: plague or panic?' *Journal of Forensic Psychiatry,* 11 (3), pp. 511–31.

Westwood, Mathew and Perkin, Corrie (2008) 'Artists jump to Henson's defence' *The Weekend Australian,* May 24–25, p. 2.

Media Glamourising of Prostitution and Other Sexually Exploitive Cultural Practices that Harm Children

Melissa Farley

The contemptuous, sexually degrading treatment of women by men is so pervasive and so mainstream in the media today that it has almost lost its ability to shock us (Herbert, 2006). The message to girls is that they '... should always be sexually available, always have sex on their minds, be willing to be dominated and even sexually aggressed against' (Merskin, 2004, p. 120).

Prostitution behaviours are part of what it means to be female today. Trained by popular western culture, girls learn to present a hypersexualised, prostitution-like version of themselves to the world. Ariel Levy described the 'imaginary licentiousness' that girls enact in order to appear grown up. One girl explained, 'Sexually, we didn't really do anything, but you wanted to *look* like you did' (Levy, 2005, p. 150).

Today, children are enacting the sex of prostitution. Casually fellating boys at parties is normative for girls, according to a recent Canadian article. One girl repeated the classic pimp's argument for prostitution, noting that if she was already fellating two or three boys every weekend at parties for free, she might as well do the same with five or six boys and get paid for it (Hanon, 2009).

Introducing children to a culture of sexual violence, web-based pornography bombards children with images of graphic and brutal exploitation of women. No hint of tenderness or intimacy is revealed in these Internet photographs. Boys who use the Internet are systematically groomed to be the next generation of pay-for-porn customers. They are also taught to normalise the buying of sex. One in three children who are online receive unwanted pornography. 'I go to web sites about racing dirt bikes,' said one boy, 'and when I'm on there pop-up ads come up with naked pictures of girls and guys' (Wolak et al., 2006).

Even though it is well established that pornography and video games powerfully influence real-life behaviour, we are told that they are mere fantasy and have nothing to do with real-life rape. But if fantasy has nothing to do with reality, why is advertising a multibillion dollar industry? In fact, advertising uses fantasy to influence reality. Twenty-five percent of all web search engine requests are for pornography, according to familysafemedia. com (2008). The 1.5 billion pornography downloads a month represent 35 per cent of all web downloads. Revenue from online pornography is greater than the revenues of the top technology companies combined: Microsoft, Google, Amazon, eBay, Yahoo!, Apple, Netflix and EarthLink (Criddle, 2008).

It is a mistake to separate the use of pornography from other sexual behaviours. Given the saturation of the Australian and US media with sexually exploitive imagery, children receive a far more intensive sex education from pornography than from parents or teachers. A video game designer explained it this way, 'We can't, on the one hand, crow about the power of software as a learning tool, and on the other hand say the immersion in realistic graphic violence has no impact on a player' (Interview with Steve Meretzky quoted in Brathwaite, 2007, p. 206).

Children live under tremendous pressure to act on the messages they see and hear in the media. Increasingly, young boys are learning to commit acts of sexual violence against girls.[1] In the following news account, one youth's imitation of the violence in Grand Theft Auto IV is illustrated.

> Sales of the video game Grand Theft Auto IV were halted in Thailand after a teenager said he had killed a taxi driver while trying to recreate a scene from the game. After the 19 year old, Polwat Chino, was said to have confessed to the killing, the police in Bangkok said the teenager 'had wanted to find out if it was as easy in real life to rob a taxi as it was in the game' (Bloom, 2008).

Grand Theft Auto IV also gives players the option of increasing their points by sexually assaulting a prostitute and then murdering her.

A Japanese videogame invites players to simulate rapes of a single mother and her two young daughters in a Tokyo subway. The game player who is described as a 'public nuisance' captures each female, raping and 'breaking each respective target' to his liking. After that, the player is instructed to move into another part of town where the game involves raping other women and children at random. The game also has a multiple-player option that provides young men the opportunity to learn gang-rape-via-videogame (Fenelly, 2009).

Prostitution is normalised for children by 'soft' or 'amateur' pornography like *Girls Gone Wild* and by videos that mainstream prostitution and prostitution-like activities. For *Girls Gone Wild* footage, Joe Francis takes his film crew to clubs where teenagers are partying. After drinking and partying, Francis persuades and entices girls into being filmed. Francis has been jailed on charges

---

1   In 2008, the Australian press reported that a group of six-year-old boys had coerced girls into prostitution-like sex acts. http://news.ninemsn.com.au/national/630867/trio-of-schoolboys-ran-sex-club

of child abuse subsequent to his production of child pornography.[2]

Sexual boundaries have disappeared on many Internet social networking sites, increasing the vulnerability of children. Popular sites MySpace, Facebook, Flickr, Stickam and Yahoo host adult pornography, child pornography, and solicitation for prostitution. MySpace, for example, lists thinly veiled prostitution advertising such as 'Find a Booty Call' (Criddle, 2008). Stickam, another socially risky website used by teenagers, encourages them to post live webcam sexual behaviors (Stone, 2007).

Espin-the-bottle, a social networking site aimed at teenagers, is advertised as a sexualised 'flirting and dating' site for those aged 13 to 57. The *Espin* site accepts advertising from companies that promote ways to help children hide their Internet use from parents. The site targets children with quizzes that encourage sexualised responses which are then posted on the site (Criddle, 2008).

Another site, MissBimbo.com, encourages girls to compete to become the 'hottest, coolest, most famous bimbo in the whole world' (Criddle, 2008). Girls are adversely impacted by images of their own sexualised commodification and by images that trivialise sexual violence (Kilbourne, 2000). They internalise media messages about themselves. The early sexualisation of girls means that sexual activity begins at a younger age, that risky sexual behaviours increase, and that pornography is considered a fun activity. Summarising these effects, physician Linnea Smith and colleagues commented that 'the media acts as an advertising agent for prostitution' (Smith, 2005, p. 40).

Sexual exploitation of girls occurs in many forms of music but the exploitation is particularly toxic in the misogynist, racist lyrics of hip-hop in which all women are considered 'ho's' and 'bitches' who deserve men's contempt and violence (American Psycholog-

---

2   See Ariel Levy (2005, pp. 7–17) for an extended description of a Joe Francis shoot. See also Associated Press (2008) 'Florida: "Wild" Girls Founder is Set Free;' CNN.com (2008) 'Spitzer escort's "Girls Gone Wild" videos surface Via Associated Press' and TMZ. com (2008) 'Ashley Dupre Gone "Wild"—Legal or Jailbait?'

ical Association, 2007; Armstrong, 2001). African-American girls have been especially harmed by rap culture which glorifies pimping and stereotypes them as hypersexual, sexually irresponsible, and uninterested in emotionally committed relationships (Davis, 2004).

Playfully imitating the commercialised hypersexualisation that they watch on the Internet, girls may be unwitting participants in their own sexual exploitation. Learning from pornography, children attempt sex that is casual, non-relational, and without consequences or commitments. Young women are taught the sexuality of prostitution which means that they ignore their own sexual feelings (or lack of them) and learn that their role is to service boyfriends who have also learned about sex via pornography. Thirteen-year-old girls who are Jenna Jameson fans attend her book tour for readings from *How to Make Love like a Porn Star* (Paul, 2005). Fifteen-year-old girls ask *CosmoGirl* sex advice columnists if they can get pregnant from anal sex—a query likely stemming from their boyfriends' pornography use. Girls assume that anal sex is as commonplace in real life as it is in pornography (*CosmoGirl*, 2007). Yet an actual response from *CosmoGirl* only addressed the physiology of anal sex. What should have been discussed was whether the relationship was egalitarian, how much choice the young woman felt she did or did not have to assert her own sexual preferences, and a consideration of the possibility that she may have been experiencing sexual coercion because her boyfriend was learning from pornography.

Today, some young women have embraced their own degrading objectification (Levy, 2005; Gold, 2007). Seeming to have abandoned the hope of real equality with men, women and girls enact prostitution. Pole dancing, once the exclusive province of women in strip clubs, has moved to women's homes and exercise classes. Lap dancing and pole dancing have become mainstreamed as women's and girls' sexuality. Classes in pole dancing are now advertised as fitness exercises to girls as young as seven (Yamine,

2007). Stripper-chic apparel mainstreams prostitution for young women and girls. In the following example from an Internet teen-dating advice column, a girl is taught how to perform a lap dance for her boyfriend:

Question: hi jen, well i have a lil problem its not really a problem but it is for me.. i wanna giove my boyfriend a lap dance, bc he wants me 2 and i think it would be fun but i cant dance and have no idea how to lap dance, i cant go and buy ne videos or ne thing bc im not 18 so i would have to use my parents credit card to buy it online and that wouldnt work and i dont wanna buy it at some store and i dont think i would be able to buy it. please help.

Answer: Hey Holly, well to give a lap dance you have to feel sexy. so wear your sexist undies and bra, and provocative clothing. you should start by giving him sexy looks and winks and little teasing kisses. its all about dominating. put on some music you can grind too. you start off infront of him and just dance kinda of dirty. if you can't dance and can't get a friend to show you, just rub yourself infront of him. spread your legs slightly and rub your chest your neck, down ur stomach and ur inner theighs. lick ur finger, look really sexy. thats when you start stripping. start with shirt. after you take it off, get on top of him and rub your chest all in his face and roll your body against his. ★he has to be sitting up★ have your hair down and flowing around, so it looks wild. and continue from there. everytime you take something off, make sure it looks sexy and rub against him like ur life depended on it. make him want you. give him a hardon by watching you strip and rub against him. get on top of him kiss down his body. do everything and anything you want. remember you are in control and thats why your making him want you. its your show, make him beg. hope i helped bye bye love Jen (Allexperts.com, 2005).

Middle school students at a 2005 career day in California were told that stripping and exotic dancing were excellent careers for girls. A job counselor explained to a group of students that strippers earn very good salaries, especially if they have breast enlargement surgery. 'For every two inches up there, it's another $50,000' he enthusiastically told the girls (Kim, 2005).

Focusing on anatomy, physiology, and pregnancy, sex educators spend too little time teaching children about non-exploitive sexuality and intimate love relationships. Much of children's sex education is left to pornographers and pimps. According to one survey, Australian teens were receiving most of their information about sex from Internet porn sites rather than from their parents or sex education programs: 97 per cent of girls, and 100 per cent of boys had viewed pornography before age fifteen (Sauers, 2007).

Yet children tell us about their need for education in how to develop intimate relationships. They don't want to know only about the anatomy and physiology of sex. An Australian boy complained that his sex education class did not teach him anything about sexual intimacy. He commented, 'They should warn you in school about how bad you feel after a one-night stand!' (Scobie, 2007).

Children today need media literacy education so that they learn to counteract toxic messages about their sexuality. It is possible to teach children how to assess the sexually exploitive messages that are lodged today in a range of technologies from video games to cell phone applications to Internet pornography. Technical and media consciousness raising are essential—first for parents themselves, and then for parents to teach children.

Media literacy resource material must include not only resources on sex stereotyping, but specific education on the damaging effects of the media's sexualisation of children with recommendations for ways to discuss these issues with children of different ages. Like parents everywhere, US President Obama worries about the flood of commercial messages that sexualise children: 'I worry that even if Michelle and I do our best to impart what we think are important values to our children, the media out there will undermine our lessons and teach them something different' (Campaign for a Commercial-Free Childhood, 2009).

Linnea Smith suggests that parents and paediatricians challenge corporations that promote the sexualisation of children (Smith et al., 2005). Other educators provide teaching models for evaluating and deconstructing common myths in the media about sexuality and love (Galician and Merskin, 2007). Media Awareness Network provides extensive resources for educating children about pornography and sexual advertising. MediaWatch offers a feminist analysis of sexism and violence in the media.

There are many tools available to decrease or eliminate the toxic intensity of media sexualisation of girls. If utilised, these resources could raise awareness about sexual exploitation, and children could grow up with a sexuality that is their own, rather than one imposed on them by a culture dominated by pimps and pornographers.

References

Allexperts.com (2005) 'Teen Dating Issues' accessed April 25, 2008 from http://en.allexperts.com/q/Teen-Dating-Issues-849/lap-dance.htm

American Psychological Association (2007) *Report of the APA Task Force on the Sexualization of Girls*. American Psychological Association, Washington DC.

Armstrong, E.G. (2001) 'Gangsta Misogyny: a content analysis of the portrayals of violence against women in rap music 1987-1993' *Journal of Criminal Justice and Popular Culture* 8 (2), pp. 96–126.

Associated Press (2008) 'Florida: "Wild" Girls Founder is Set Free' *New York Times,* March 13 accessed March 27, 2008 from http://www.nytimes.com/2008/03/13/

us/13brfs8216WILD8217_BRF.html?scp=13&sq=&st=nyt

Bloom, Julie (2008) 'Arts, Briefly' *New York Times,* August 5,
http://www.nytimes.com/2008/08/05/arts/05arts-SALEOF
GRANDT_BRF.html

Brathwaite, Brenda. (2007) *Sex in Video Games.* Charles River
Media, Boston.

Campaign for a Commercial-Free Childhood (2009) accessed May
11, 2009 from http://www.commercialfreechildhood.org/

CNN.com (2008) 'Spitzer escort's "Girls Gone Wild" videos
surface via Associated Press accessed April 4, 2008 from http://
www.cnn.com/2008/US/03/18/dupree.girls.gone.wild.ap/
index.html

CosmoGirl (2007) Accessed April 19, 2008 from http://www.
cosmogirl.com/lifeadvice/sex-questions/talk-about-sex-oct07

Criddle, Linda (2008) 'Human trafficking and the Internet'
accessed April 26, 2008 from www.look-both-ways.com

Davis, Thulani (2004) 'New study on "hip-hop sexuality"
finds anti-woman strain even among young women' *Village
Voice*, March 17 accessed May 22, 2005 from http://www.
villagevoice.com/issues/0411/davis.php

Familysafemedia.com (2008) accessed April 26, 2008 from
http://familysafemedia.com/

Fenelly, Gary (2009) 'Exclusive: Amazon selling rape simulation
game' *Belfast Telegraph,* February 12, 2009, accessed February
12, 2009 from http://www.belfasttelegraph.co.uk/news/local-
national/amazon-selling-3d-rape-simulator-game-14183546.
html

Galician, Mary-Lou and Merskin, Debra L. (2007) *Critical
Thinking about Sex, Love, and Romance in the Mass Media.*
Lawrence Erlbaum, Mahwah, NJ.

Gold, G.K. (2007) 'What is liberation? Feminism past, present
and future' accessed January 1, 2007 from http://sisyphe.org/
article.php3?id_article=2551

127

Hanon, A. (2009) 'Teen girls trading sex for favours' *Edmonton Sun,* April 1, 2009, http://cnews.canoe.ca/CNEWS/Canada/2009/04/01/8959961-sun.html

Herbert, Bob (2006) 'Why Aren't We Shocked?' *New York Times*, October 16 accessed February 2, 2007 from http://select.nytimes.com/2006/10/16/opinion/16herbert.html?hp

Kilbourne, Jean (2000) 'Killing us Softly: Advertising's Image of Women' accessed March 22, 2008 from http://www.mediaed.org/videos/MediaGenderAnd Diversity/KillingUsSoftly3

Kim, Ryan (2005) 'Bump, grind your way to riches, students told' *San Francisco Chronicle,* January 14 accessed January 14, 2005 from http://www.fradical.com/Pimping_at_school_career_day.htm

Levin, Diane (2008) 'So Sexy So Soon: The Sexualization of Childhood' speech given at Consuming Kids: The Sexualization of Children and Other Commercial Calamities. Campaign for a Commerical-Free Childhood 6th Summit, Boston, April 3-5, 2008.

Levy, Ariel (2005) *Female Chauvinist Pigs: Women and the Rise of Raunch Culture.* Free Press, New York.

Media Awareness Network (2008) http://www.media-awareness.ca/english/tools/main_search/search_results.cfm accessed April 13, 2008.

MediaWatch (2008) http://www.mediawatch.com accessed April 13, 2008.

Merskin, Debra L. (2004) 'Reviving Lolita? A Media Literacy Examination of Sexual Portrayals of Girls in Fashion Advertising' *American Behavioral Scientist* 48(1), pp. 119–129.

Paul, Pamela (2005) *Pornified; How Pornography is Transforming Our Lives, Our Relationships, and our Families.*Times Books, New York.

Sauers, Joan (2007) *Sex Lives of Australian Teenagers.* Random House, Sydney and New York.

Scobie, C. (2007) 'Wild Things' *The Bulletin*, Australia, June 2.

Smith, Linnea, Herman-Giddens, M.E. and Everette, V.D. (2005) 'Commercial Sexual Exploitation of Children in Advertising' in Sharon W. Cooper, Richard J. Estes, Angelo P. Giardino, Nancy D. Kellogg, and Victor I. Vieth (Eds) *Medical, Legal, and Social Science Aspects of Child Sexual Exploitation: A Comprehensive Review of Pornography, Prostitution, and Internet Crimes, Volumes 1 and 2,* GW Medical Publishing, St Louis.

Stone, B. (2007) 'Using Web Cams but Few Inhibitions, the Young Turn to risky Social Sites' *New York Times,* January 2 accessed June 20, 2007 from http://www.nytimes.com/2007/01/02/technology/02net.html?_r=1&ref=business&oref=slogin.

TMZ.com (2008) 'Ashley Dupre Gone "Wild" - Legal or Jailbait?' accessed April 4, 2008 from http://www.tmz.com/2008/03/19/ashley-dupre-gone-wild-legal-or-jailbait/

Wolak, J., Mitchell, K., and Finkelhor, D. (2006) 'Online Victimization of Youth: Five Years Later' National Center for Missing and Exploited Children. Report #07-06-025. Alexandria, VA.

Yamine, E. (2007) 'Girls gaining fitness or losing innocence?' *Daily Telegraph*, Sydney October 8 accessed February 24, 2008 from http://www.news.com.au/story/0,23599,22545912-2,00.html

The Harmful Medicalisation of Sexualised Girls

Renate Klein

Social scripts

It is almost unavoidable these days for girls not to be drawn into the sexualisation industry. From billboards on their way to school to the ubiquitous TVs at home, girls are bombarded with multimedia messages about seductive looks and behaviours. They spend a large part of their days and nights in cyberspace using msn, meebo chatrooms, exploring the 'hottest bands, sexiest celebs and fresh new videos' on bebo and YouTube and updating their Facebook pages which, if they so wish (or are not careful), can be shared with the whole world. Without looking for it, pornography is just a click away. It's not surprising then that surrounded by so much grown-up stuff, many girls perform these roles in real life as they do in cyberspace where their looks and identities need not match their 'real' selves.[1]

The social script tells girls that in real life and cyber life they must attract boys. There is nothing new about this message, but what has changed over the past years is that the pressure to attract boys is now applied at an increasingly younger age. So is objectification: many young girls try to be thin and sexy, strut and pose like pole

---

1 For a detailed analysis on the problems with multiple identities and disembodiment in post-modern cyberage see Klein (1996, 1999). Norman Doidge (2007) writes about net pornography's influence on the plastic minds of young men (p. 103).

dancers, and wear 'I'm a Pornstar' T–shirts in order to be popular with boys.

Being sexualised early leads to sexual behaviours. Servicing boys with oral sex is increasingly common and discussed in girls' magazines (Levy, 2005; Tankard Reist and Maggie Hamilton, this volume). Upgrading to the 'real' thing—sexual intercourse—is becoming normalised and perceived by many—girls and boys—as 'no big deal' and a necessary ingredient of being 'cool.'

Sex for adults has long had its own 'health' industry. This has now been extended to girls—a market expansion surely applauded by pharmaceutical companies. Considering having sex means having to deal with contraception, a possible sexually transmitted infection, a possible pregnancy, a possible child, a possible abortion. In a short time, a girl may thus not only be sexualised, but *medicalised* and in the hands of multiple 'experts.'

The following scenario illustrates my concerns.

> Emma, an Australian girl, aged 14, struggles over her popularity with the boys in her class. She thinks she's too fat and her mother doesn't buy her the right clothes. She has taken to throwing up after eating, but is pleased when her emulating of *Dolly's* beauty advice gets her a boyfriend. She is keen on having the three Gardasil injections so she won't get cervical cancer from sex—that's what she has been told this vaccine does.

> The severe body rash and fatigue she develops after the second injection doesn't help her confidence but nevertheless, she soon engages in sex, without condoms or contraception (the boyfriend didn't want the former and Emma was too embarrassed to ask her mother for help with getting a script for the pill).

> The sex wasn't what she had imagined, the boy dumps her, she puts on weight again and feels distressed. The rash over her whole body gets worse including blisters after the

third Gardasil injection. She is exhausted most of the time. Her once excellent school results plummet which leads to fights at home.

She panics when her period hasn't arrived for the second time (the first time she ignored it), breaks down and tells her parents. Her mother takes her to a clinic where she is informed that her daughter who is eight weeks pregnant qualifies for a 'medical' abortion as she appears by now to be severely depressed (one of the indications for the limited use of the abortion pill, RU486, in Australia). The same day, Emma is given three pills and is told to come back two days later for the second part of the abortion (the prostaglandin). She becomes violently ill with stomach cramps and nausea. She passes the foetus that, although tiny, is quite well formed. This really upsets her. When the bleeding hasn't stopped after two weeks she needs a D&C to remove the remaining foetal tissue. She is so scared that she asks for a general anaesthetic that makes her very sick when she wakes up. She has trouble sleeping and spends hours crying in her room.

By this time she is on an SSRI antidepressant. At school she has become the butt of jokes and gossip (including in cyberspace). She responds with outbursts of temper alternating with feelings of loneliness and bottomless despair. She sees her future as bleak, not worth living for. And she still has the rash all over her body. She thinks all of this must be her own fault and believes she is a total failure. Her mother is making lots of medical appointments for her and she is seeing a psychiatrist.

I sincerely hope that there will never be an 'Emma' who has to experience all parts of this unfortunate scenario. But this chain of events depicts the very real damage that early sexualisation followed by medicalisation can do to girls. I might have added self-harm (cutting) and a suicide attempt to 'Emma's' story. Or the development of a serious eating disorder. An antipsychotic medication might have been prescribed in addition to her antidepressants. And, as it happened in the real life story of a sixteen-year-old girl known to me who ended up deeply distressed after early sex, a pregnancy and an abortion, and was put on multiple drugs, 'Emma' might have developed seizures and be diagnosed with schizophrenia within three years from these events. The 'sickness industry' acquires young consumers and keeps them for life (see Moynihan and Cassels, 2005). Importantly, such stories are not discussed in public but remain agonisingly hidden in families' private lives.

Girls as medical consumers

Some readers might argue that this scenario and my assumptions about medicalisation as a consequence of early sexualisation are exaggerated.[2] How many fourteen-year-olds really do have sex? Many will just be talking about it, or pretending that they are doing it. This may be so, but it doesn't invalidate my point.[3] The medical industry gets a hold on young girls as *new consumers* whether or not they are already engaging in sex.

The so-called cervical cancer vaccines Gardasil and Cervarix are a case in point. They are experimental vaccines against two strains

---

2   Others might argue that some medications are life-savers—true—and that I am 'doctor bashing'—not true. Most of us need good medical care at some point in our lives and this may include medication. And there are many doctors who are wary of 'Big Pharma' and over-prescribing. My argument is that when an obligatory 'outsourcing' of body/mind problems starts already in childhood, a critical distance to commodification and (over)medicalisation might never be developed.

3   There are no reliable data on the onset of sexual activity in western countries. The 2005 Adolescent Health Cohort Study in the State of Victoria found that 'One in four Year 10 students [aged 15] and one in two Year 12 students [aged 17] have had sexual intercourse' (in ARCSHS, 2005 p. 12). Anecdotal data from Joan Sauers' 2006 web questionnaire of 300 Australian teenagers suggests that by the age of fifteen, one in five boys and one in six girls has had sexual intercourse (Sauers, 2007). Rachel Skinner has found a median age of fourteen for first experience of intercourse in her study of 68 teenage girls aged fourteen to nineteen in Perth. Skinner reports that 'teenage girls regret having sex earlier' and that they cite 'peer pressure, coercion from sexual partners and being drunk' as common reasons for 'premature and unwanted first experience of sexual intercourse' (in Insciences, May 19, 2009).

of the human papillomavirus (HPV) that are associated with many, but not all cases of cervical cancer (Tankard Reist and Klein, 2007; Klein and Tankard Reist, 2007; Klein, 2008d, 2009). There are over 100 strains of HPV and 80 per cent of people have the virus at some point in their lives.[4] The good news is that in 90 per cent of those who acquire HPV a healthy immune system disappears the virus infection in one to two years and no abnormal cells, let alone cancer, will develop (Lippman et al., 2007). The HPV vaccines remain unproven; it will be many years, if ever, before scientists are able to show whether they do indeed prevent cervical cancer as most cancers take ten to twenty years or longer to develop (Sawaya and Smith McCune, 2007). Meanwhile the vaccine manufacturers are raking in millions.

When girls as young as nine[5] are told they need this vaccine so that when they have sex in the future they will not get cervical cancer, they learn that their bodies can only avert disease with the help of a magic bullet from a medical expert. This is especially so when the message is bundled up with the politics of fear: girls are urged to get a vaccine for a disease the great majority will never get.[6] It is capitalism generating new markets by commodifying, privatising and separating out girls' body parts and offering them medical solutions to keep them healthy (see Hawthorne, 2008). Thus girls internalise early that their health is something that needs to be outsourced (an early gene test for family breast cancer or diabetes?). They can't stay healthy by themselves. And, importantly, they are reassured that by

---

4 There are children already born with an HPV infection which gradually disappears (Castellsague et al., 2009). It is sexual intercourse that makes females especially vulnerable to sexual transmission from males. The many strains of the human papillomavirus and their behaviour is far from being fully understood.

5 In 2006, Merck & Co in the USA and Commonwealth Serum Laboratories (CSL) in Australia achieved FDA and TGA approval for Gardasil to be administered to girls as young as nine although fewer than 1,200 girls under sixteen were included in Merck's studies (see Lippman et al., 2007).

6 In western countries the incidence of women dying from cervical cancer is steadily declining. According to a WHO/ICO report, in 2006, 249 women died in Australia and cervical cancer mortality ranks seventeen out of all 23 listed cancers (WHO/ICO, 2007, p. 8). While every death is a tragedy, pre-cancerous cells are detected through screening programs.

going to an expert, they are making a 'choice' for good health. It's the new version of being in control in the 21st century: 'I hand over my body to you, the expert, but I do so because I want to; it is my choice.[7] And I am being responsible.' Sadly, the seemingly good idea of personal responsibility can be turned on its head. If adverse effects occur they are often blamed on the individual: 'she had an undiagnosed genetic precondition…it's not the medication's fault.'

The disappearance of critical voices

What such early medicalisation does is prevent girls from developing a sense of a healthy embodied self. Sexualisation has already made many of them dissatisfied with their 'outside' bodies; medicalisation now colonises their 'inside' bodies—perfect material for the varieties of medical specialists who will take ownership of women's reproductive lives when they become pregnant, are pressured to agree that their foetus needs to be tested for any 'defects' and then possibly scared into a difficult late-term abortion (Tankard Reist, 2006). Or, if a woman can't get pregnant, ahead lie donor insemination and then in-vitro fertilisation (IVF) where she will be given dangerous hormone-like drugs to assist the procedures. She might also be faced with the 'choice' of her own eggs, her own womb—or those of other women: an egg 'donor' and a so-called surrogate mother.[8]

For women who have been instructed to treat their body parts like household items in need of repair since they were young girls, such decisions will seem quite normal.

Unlike in the late 1960s to the mid-1990s when women's health issues were frequently and critically discussed in the mainstream

---

7   I have long been a critic of the concept of 'choice.' True choice should be between choosing an apple cake or a chocolate cake and not between two options that are both problematic and may vary only by degree. If there is truly no better alternative then what you make is a difficult 'decision'—not a happy 'choice.'

8   For a detailed discussion of the problems with reproductive technologies see Klein, 2008c.

media,[9] these days the topic has all but disappeared. Or, if it is mentioned, it is to glowingly promote a new product as in the case of the 'cervical cancer' vaccines. In the case of contraception, this issue too has receded from public discussion: it is now a private matter to be discussed in the GP's office or the Family Planning Clinic. 'Mustn't get pregnant' is the only instruction. The general public assumes that a cafeteria of contraceptive 'choices' is on offer: all efficient, easy to use and without problems. The minipill? A patch slapped on to your thigh? A pill called 'Lybrel' to get rid of messy periods altogether?[10] A rod implanted in your arm that 'protects' you for three years (Monteiro-Dantas, 2007; Klein, 2008b)?[11] An IUD with or without hormones? Or the resurrected Depo Provera injection that lasts three months (and girls are not told that they'll lose bone mass they won't ever fully recover, see Klein, 2008a).[12]

Adverse effects aren't mentioned: there is meant to be a 'quick fix' for every issue at hand and dangers are rarely mentioned. And many girls know so little about their bodies that they can't be bothered with details, including information about possible health problems that might arise after many years' exposure to potent hormone-like drugs. When they are worried, for instance after unprotected sex or when a condom breaks, they will go to the pharmacy for the over-the-counter morning-after pill. Or be taken by their school, as was exposed in 2007 in Melbourne when

---

9 The international Women's Health Movement burst on the scene with books such as *Our Bodies Ourselves* (Boston Women's Health Collective, 1969); *Men Who Control Women's Health* (Scully, 1980/1992); *How to Stay out of the Gynecologist's Office* (LA Feminist Women's Health Center, 1981). The idea was for women to become holistic experts on our own health and lives.

10 At the time of writing (June 2009), Lybrel is not available in Australia but can be obtained in New Zealand, the USA and Europe.

11 A particular harrowing use of Implanon came to light in 2008 in Australia when a 52-year-old health worker took a fourteen-year-old girl to the local health clinic to have Implanon inserted before he started sexually abusing her. As Melinda Tankard Reist commented: 'This is not about freedom of sexual expression. It is about branding girls for sex' (May 6, 2008).

12 Hormonal contraception for men is as far away as ever. Despite a number of trials, men simply won't put up with side effects. Women continue to do so.

girls as young as thirteen were taken by their teachers 'to get the "morning-after" pill without parents being told' (in Houlihan, 2007). Most likely, they won't be told that multiple exposures to one type of morning-after pill that uses Levonorgestrel (the synthetic progesterone used in Implanon) may triple their risk for multiple sclerosis and lead to an increased risk of breast cancer (Bennett and Pope, 2008, p. 275).

Promoting ignorance is early indoctrination into 'naturally' putting up with nausea, bleeding, weight gain, headaches, disturbance of the metabolism of nutrients, higher risk of strokes, heart attacks and cancer—all 'side effects' of contraceptives—in order to be sexually available 24/7 and reduce the chance of an unintended pregnancy. The highly accessible book *The Pill. Are You Sure It's for You?* (2008) by Jane Bennett and Alexandra Pope is countering this information gap in the available literature and should be widely read. Not only do the authors discuss pros and cons of the pill and other contraceptives in great detail without shying away from their serious adverse effects, they urge girls and women to get in touch with their own bodies and not continue to be the 'canaries in the mine' for the increasing chemical load added to their bodies. An informative chapter introduces fertility awareness methods and how they can become an empowering part of girls' and women's lives. They also make the insightful comment that '[B]ooks on relationships and sexuality generally don't discuss contraception' but that '[If] you make these choices haphazardly or unconsciously—by following the crowd or based on insufficient advice—then this can lead to resentment and distance in your sexual relationship rather than sexual intimacy' (p. 269). And, I would add, to severely compromised health.

Another example of insufficient—or wrong—advice is the normalisation of chemical abortion. When RU 486/prostaglandin abortion is promoted, it is said to be 'easy' and 'natural.' Apparent 'power' is conferred to a girl or woman because it is she who swallows three pills of mifepristone (and two days later takes the prostaglandin). It is not only unfair but dangerous to suggest this, because once the drugs are in her body, she has no control over whether she might be one of those girls or women who experience terrible nausea, vomiting, cramping and bleeding for up to six weeks, or worse (Klein, Raymond and Dumble, 1991; Klein 2006; for a harrowing account of an RU 486 abortion, see Dworkin-McDaniel, 2007). Because abortion is now seen as no big deal—and in Australia independent counselling before making a decision to terminate a pregnancy is not thought to be important—many girls aren't even given the opportunity to consider if maybe, just maybe, they should at least try to find out what resources might be available if they decided to have the baby (see Tankard Reist, 2000).

Chemical citizenship

No wonder many girls who have to cope with the multiple de-mands of living in the sexualised real and cyberworld and who experience early medicalisation feel disconnected from themselves and begin to act strangely. Sometimes support is being offered by family doctors and a girl might find a sensitive counsellor to talk through the multifaceted problems upsetting her. But all too often she soon finds herself diagnosed with 'depression' and put on antidepressants. Indeed, these drugs have become so 'ordinary' and are used by so many people that hardly anyone questions their use.[13] But they are not without danger. The SSRI antidepressant Zoloft, in particular, has been linked to an increase in suicidal thinking and behaviour when administered to children and adolescents. Following the FDA, in 2004, the Australian Adverse Drug Reactions Advisory Committee (ADRAC) issued a warning about the off-label use of selective serotonin reuptake inhibitors (SSRIs) in children and adolescents under eighteen years. ADRAC states that they are not approved for the treatment of depression in these age groups and have been associated with increased numbers of

13   Julie-Anne Davis reports that in 2007 'More than twelve million SSRI anti-depressant scripts were subsidised by the Pharmaceutical Benefits Scheme' (November 1–2, 2008b, p. 9).

suicide and self-harm attempts (www.tga.gov.au/adr/adrac_ssri. htm). In spite of these warnings, off-label prescription for children continues and, as in the case of a fourteen-year-old girl, can result in suicide attempts (see Davis, 2008a, p. 28).

While public awareness campaigns about mental health issues have done much over the last decade to remove the stigma from people with serious mental disorders, they have, inadvertently perhaps, contributed to a far too high acceptance that feeling sad, in turmoil after suffering loss or experiencing sexual assault, and, in the case of girls suffering from sexualisation's excesses and feeling anxious and depressed, amounts to 'mental illness' and must be medicated. Sadness, as Janet Stoppard and Linda M. McMullen suggest (2003) needs to be seen within a social context rather than turning the young into 'chemical citizens' at an early age.[14] Adelaide child psychiatrist Jon Jureidini, a long-term critic of inappropriate prescribing of antidepressants, believes that depression in children, adolescents and young adults can be safely treated '[T]hrough a combination of "watchful waiting" and physical and emotional rehabilitation…without reliance on medication or psychotherapy' (2009, p. 275).

It is very worrisome to foreshadow the health of women at midlife after they may have faced, as young women, various chemical assaults from the HPV vaccine, the contraceptive pill, the morning-after pill, perhaps the abortion pill RU 486, maybe antidepressants, fertility stimulating hormone-like drugs, and later hormone replacement therapy (HRT). Abigail Bray's term 'chemical citizen' couldn't be more fitting: add some of the recreational drugs that many adolescents ply themselves with regularly and you don't need to be scaremongering to worry how the immune system will cope—or not—with such overload. Indeed it is a 'chemical economy of control' (Bray, 2009, p. 98) that is taking over our lives.

---

14   I thank Abigail Bray for this expression taken from her essay 'Chemical Control™®: From the Cane to the Pill' (2009) in which she argues that drugs like Ritalin and antidepressants have replaced the cane in disciplining children.

The politics of fear

An adverse effect of both antidepressants and hormonal contraception is weight gain which makes the medicalisation/sexualisation nexus especially obvious. To be thin and weightless is the ideal, to be 'fat' even if only in a girl's own mind, can lead to extreme self-loathing. Unfortunately, yet another aspect of the medicalisation of children comes into play here and it arrives in our lives care of our own health authorities. For at least a decade we have now heard that an obesity epidemic is nigh in Australia and the UK and that the best way to measure obesity is the Body Mass Index (BMI) that is calculated using a mathematical formulation of weight and height. Undoubtedly, many children don't get much exercise when they remain indoors and are glued to their computers, and the ads for junk food still recruit many customers (especially when it is cheaper than healthy food). Government campaigns on 'healthy living' are to be welcomed (and should include subsidies to organic farmers). What is less welcome is the far too uncritical assumption that your BMI determines whether you are in the 'obese' category and at risk of suffering from diabetes and heart disease. Such scaremongering also stigmatises children who are indeed overweight as 'weak-willed, ugly and awkward' (O'Dea, 2005, p. 259). It reaches problematic proportions when health authorities threaten to seize overweight kids from their parents (Rose, 2009). Joanne Ikeda and colleagues question whether BMI screening in British schools is 'helpful or harmful' (2006, p. 761). Child health researcher Jennifer O'Dea cautions to 'First, do no harm' in the prevention of child obesity (2005, p. 259). As she put it to a Parliamentary Senate Inquiry into Obesity (2008):

> There's a lot of money to be made out of the idea that every Australian man, woman, child and dog could lose some weight…There's a lot of profit and influence and power and ego involved in these careers in obesity, and in selling products, pills, formulas, pharmaceuticals, books and surgery promoting weight loss (in Guilliatt, 2009, p. 21).

141

A perfect example of how well meant and important concerns about children's wellbeing are turned into the latest arena of personalised medical intervention (possibly coupled with a test for a genetic disposition to obesity). This has serious consequences for a child's developing relationship with her or his body. As Susie Orbach puts it succinctly: 'The body is experienced as menace' (2009, p. 111).

Fast forward to a healthy life

With medicalisation as a result of early sexualisation girls are fast forwarded into the adult consumer world of the medical 'choice' industry. This is where capitalism meets—and exploits—liberal (feminist) dreams of girl power.

If we don't want young girls to succumb to the politics of fear under the false guise of 'it's my responsibility and my choice,' we need to instil a healthy dose of scepticism. The medical industry doesn't always know best; it might not be the first option to explore. We are ourselves, our bodies and minds, and children must not be robbed of the time it takes to get to know—and appreciate—themselves. And no one needs to be 'perfect'—whatever 'perfect' might be.

There is a wealth of knowledge about 'good living' passed on in families from generation to generation, often by women who know lots about home remedies and nutrition. Health and wellbeing has to be the starting point, rather than screening or testing for the absence of disease. Providing information to young women (and men) about how to eat well, engage in physical activities, not smoke, drink in moderation (if they must), and look for the positives in life rather than the negatives, so that their immune system is strong, would be a better strategy than uncritically inducting them into the medical industry. Some might say that such messages will fall on deaf ears but I suggest we should never give up trying to inform before we reach for the pill—or the syringe as it were with the HPV vaccines mentioned earlier. At least the girls would be spared the serious adverse effects these vaccines can have for some,[15] and not become obedient consumers of the latest medical miracle before they are teenagers—many won't even have started menstruation.[16]

As adults we have a responsibility to pass on to young women and men that they need to critically assess new 'miracle' technological, medical, and chemical fixes. This can start at an early age in schools where, in courses such as Human Relationships, they learn about issues of power and dominance and what makes boys respect girls and vice versa. In this way they learn about confidence, self-worth, self-love and integrity of body and soul which has to come from the inside, not from others, even if they present as friendly helpers. The Australian Government's announcement in April 2009 that it is putting nine million dollars into 'Respectful Relationships programs' for 'mainstream school settings [that] will reach up to 8,000 young people over a period of five years' is a step in the right direction (Australian Government, 2009). When the topic of sex is raised in these discussions, the teachers must get the message across that it is perfectly okay to say 'no'—and that this is a good decision,

---

15   Adverse effects after Gardasil injections include difficulty walking, disorientation, dizziness, neurological disorders, seizures, pancreatitis, Guillain-Barré Syndrome, hyperventilation, bronchospasms, pallor, tinnitus, arthralgia (joint pains), cardiac problems and anaphylactic shock. As of April 2009, a total of 1,304 adverse reactions had been reported in Australia and by May 2009 over 16,000 in the USA (reports represent only between one and ten per cent of all adverse reactions). In the USA, by May 2009, 47 deaths have been associated with the HPV vaccine Gardasil: four times the number of deaths associated with Menactra (a vaccine against meningococcal) (for details see www.nvic.org/Downloads/NVICGardasilvsMenactraVAERSReportFeb-2009u.aspx). The vaccine manufacturers maintain that Gardasil is safe. For some of the deaths of healthy US teenagers from cardiac problems the suggestion has been that these girls might have suffered from an undiagnosed weakness (eg a heart murmur). For first hand accounts of girls' vaccination stories, see http://womenhurtbymedicine.wordpress.com/

16   Gardasil may interact with the menstrual cycle. It is also not recommended for pregnant women but there have been reports of spontaneous abortions and foetal abnormalities when pregnant women were inadvertently injected with Gardasil during the trials. Merck has set up a registry to follow pregnant women who have received Gardasil. It is unknown if fertility will be affected. http://www.merckpregnancyregistries.com/gardasil.html

not one they should be penalised for (see Clive Hamilton, this volume). They also have the right to know that multiple casual sex partners and hook ups can lead to negative emotional and physical health outcomes. And when it is appropriate that contraception is discussed, the young women (and men) must be given proper information including an introduction into the powerful actions of the sex hormones oestrogen and progesterone.

If girls—and boys—have such an informed start in life, they might be able to better deal with the challenging world around them. They might begin to like their Real Bodies. Indeed, the girls might one day join together, just as the women did in the 1960s, in a 21st century version of the Women's Liberation Movement, and in ways that fit the current times, demand to be liberated from toxic media, chemical citizenship and neoliberal consumerism. By rejecting both early sexualisation and medicalisation, both girls and boys will have a greater chance of a good life. Hopefully, the inspiring words about 'Body Power! by Elizabeth Reid Boyd and Abigail Bray in *Body Talk* (2005) will be listened to (p. 90):

> It's time to celebrate our bodies and not waste our time trashing ourselves for not measuring up, for not being perfect. It's time that we celebrated being strong and healthy and intelligent and creative. It's time we started to enjoy being inside our own skin, eating because we are really hungry, exercising because we love the feeling of power it gives us.

> Imagine the things you could do, all the energy you'd have if you didn't waste your health and time on trying to measure up. You'd experience so much freedom. You'd experience a pure and powerful joy in your own body, whatever size it might be. Free yourself. Only you can do it. No one else but you is in charge of your liberation.

References

Australian Adverse Drug Reactions Advisory Committee (2004) 'Use of SSRI antidepressants in children and adolescents' www.tga.gov.au/adr/adrac_ssri.htm

Australian Government (2009) 'Time for Action: The National Council's Plan for Australia to Reduce Violence against Women and their Children' April 29, http://www.fahcsia.gov.au/sa/women/pubs/violence/np_time_for_action/national_plan/Documents/The_Plan.pdf

Australian Research Centre for Sex Health and Society (ARCSHS) (2005) The Sexual and Reproductive Health of Young Victorians. Unpublished data. www.fpv.org.au/pdfs/HReport2_02Dec2005.pdf

Bennett, Jane and Alexandra Pope (2008) *The Pill. Are You Sure It's for You*? Allen & Unwin, Sydney.

Boston Women's Health Collective (1969). *Our Bodies Ourselves*. Simon and Schuster, New York.

Bray, Abigail (2009) 'Chemical Control™®: From the Cane to the Pill' in David Savat and Mark Poster (Eds) *Deleuze and New Technology*. Edinburgh University Press, Edinburgh, pp. 82–103.

Doidge, Norman (2007) *The Brain that Changes Itself*. Scribe Publications, Melbourne.

Castellsague, Xavier, Teresa Drudis, Maria Paz Canadas et al. (2009) 'Human Papillomavirus (HPV) infection in pregnant women and mother-to-child transmission of genital HPV genotypes: a prospective study in Spain' *BMC Infectious Diseases*, 9:74, http://www.biomedcentral.com/1471-2334/9/74/abstract

Davis, Julie-Anne (2008a) 'Suicide attempt a depressing drug side effect' *The Weekend Australian,* September 20-21, Inquirer, p. 28.

Davis, Julie-Anne (2008b) 'Probe into anti-depressants being conducted "in secret"' *The Weekend Australian,* November 1–2, The Nation, p. 9.

Dworkin-McDaniel, Norine (2007) 'I was betrayed by a pill' *Marie-Claire*, USA, July, http://www.marieclaire.com/sex-love/relationship-issues/articles/abortion-pill

Guilliatt, Richard (2009) 'Off the Scale' *The Weekend Australian Magazine*, May 9–10, pp. 19–25.

Hawthorne, Susan (2008) 'Somatic Piracy and BioPhallacies: Separation, Violence and Biotech Fundamentalism' *Women's Studies International Forum* 31 (4), July-August, pp. 308–318.

Houlihan, Liam (2007) 'School Pill Run' *Sunday Herald Sun*, March 25, http://www.acl.org.au/qld/browse.stw?article_id=14007

Ikeda, Joanne, P., Patricia Crawford and Gail Woodward-Lopez (2006) 'BMI screening in schools: helpful or harmful' *Health Education Research* 21 (6), pp. 761–769.

Insciences Organisation (2009) 'New study finds teen girls regret having sex earlier' May 19, http://insciences.org/article.php?article_id=5101

Jureidini, Jon (2009) 'How do we safely treat depression in children, adolescents and young adults?' *Drug Safety* 32(4), pp. 275–282.

Klein, Renate, Janice Raymond and Lynette Dumble (1991) *RU 486: Misconceptions, Myths and Morals*. Spinifex Press, Melbourne.

Klein, Renate (1996) '(Dead) Bodies Floating in Cyberspace: Post-modernism and the Dismemberment of Women' in Diane Bell and Renate Klein (Eds) *Radically Speaking: Feminism Reclaimed*. Spinifex Press, Melbourne, pp. 346–358.

Klein, Renate (1999) 'The Politics of Cyberfeminism: If I'm a Cyborg rather than a Goddess will Patriarchy go away' in Susan Hawthorne and Renate Klein (Eds) *Cyberfeminism. Connectivity, Critique, Creativity*. Spinifex Press, Melbourne, pp. 185–212.

Klein, Renate (2006) 'Submission to Senate Inquiry Repeal of Ministerial responsibility for approval of RU486, Bill 2005' January 15. www.aph.gov.au/senate/committee/clac_ctte/completed_inquiries/2004-07/ru486/submissions/sub605.pdf

Klein, Renate and Melinda Tankard Reist (2007) 'Gardasil: we must not ignore the risks' *On Line Opinion* June 1. www.onlineopinion.com.au/view.asp?article=5917&page=2

Klein, Renate (2008a) 'Depo Provera—the shot that lingers' *Living Wisdom* 6 (1) pp. 42–45.

Klein, Renate (2008b) 'Implanon: just slip it in?' May 6 *On Line Opinion*, http://www.onlineopinion.com.au/view. asp?article=7331

Klein, Renate (2008c) 'From test-tube women to bodies without women' *Women's Studies International Forum* 31(3) pp. 157–175.

Klein, Renate (2008d) 'The Gardasil "miracle" coming undone?' *On Line Opinion* August 21, http://www.onlineopinion.com. au/view.asp?article=7786

Klein, Renate (2009) 'Gardasil: The denial continues' *On Line Opinion* June 30, http://www.onlineopinion.com.au/view. asp?article=9112

LA Feminist Women's Health Center (1981) *How to Stay out of the Gynecologist's Office*. Peace Press, Culver City, CA.

Lippman, Abby, Ryan Melnychuk, Carolyn Shimmin and Madeline Boscoe (2007) 'Human papillomavirus, vaccines and women's health: questions and cautions' *Canadian Medical Association Journal* 177 (5), pp. 484–487 available at http:// www.cmaj.ca/content/vol177/issue5/

Monteiro-Dantas, Cecilia, Ximena Espejo-Arce et al. (2007). 'A three-year longitudinal evaluation of the forearm bone density of users of etonogestrel- and levonorgestrel-releasing contraceptive Implants' *Reproductive Health* 4 (11). http://www. pubmedcentral.nih.gov/articlerender.fcgi?pmid=17997844

Moynihan, Ray and Alan Cassels (2005) *Selling Sickness. How Drug Companies Are Turning Us All into Patients*. Allen & Unwin, Sydney.

O'Dea, Jennifer A. (2005) 'Prevention of child obesity: "First, do no harm"' *Health Education Research* 20 (2), pp. 259–265.

Orbach, Susie (2009) *Bodies*. Profile Books, London.

Reid Boyd, Elizabeth and Abigail Bray (2005) *Body Talk: A Power Guide for Girls*. Hodder Headline, Sydney.

Rose, Danny (2009) 'Call in DoCS for overweight kids: doctor' February 1, http://news.ninemsn.com.au/health/736283/call-in-docs-for-overweight-kids-doctor/?rss=yes

Sauers, Joan (2007) *Sex Lives of Australian Teenagers,* Random House Australia, Sydney.

Sawaya, George and Karen Smith-McCune (2007) 'HPV Vaccination—More Answers, More Questions' *New England Journal of Medicine* 356 (19), pp. 1991–1993 available at http://content.nejm.org/cgi/content/full/356/19/1991

Scully, Diana (1980/1994) *Men Who Control Women's Health. The Miseducation of Obstetrician-Gynecologists*. Houghton Mifflin, New York; Athene Series, Teachers College Press, New York.

Stoppard, Janet M. and Linda M. McMullen (2003). *Situating Sadness: Women and Depression in Social Context*. New York University Press: New York.

Tankard Reist, Melinda (2000) *Giving Sorrow Words: Women's Stories of Grief After Abortion*. Duffy & Snellgrove, Sydney.

Tankard Reist, Melinda (2006) *Defiant Birth: Women Who Resist Medical Eugenics*. Spinifex Press, Melbourne.

Tankard Reist, Melinda (2008) 'Branding girls for s*x' May 6 www.onlineopinion.com.au/view.asp?article=7314

Tankard Reist, Melinda and Renate Klein (2007) 'Why are we experimenting with drugs on Australian girls? The Gardasil program may benefit only drug company shareholders' *The Age*, May 25, Melbourne. http://www.theage.com.au/news/opinion/why-are-we-experimenting-with-drugs-on-girls/2007/05/24/1179601570922.html

WHO/ICO Information Centre on HPV and Cervical Cancer (2007) Human Papillomavirus and Cervical Cancer. Summary Report. http://www.who.int/hpvcentre/statistics/dynamic/ico/summaryreportsselect.cfm

Sexualised and Trivialised: Making Equality Impossible

Betty McLellan

Promoters of the sexualisation of women and girls tell us that it is a matter of personal, individual choice. But those of us with a long-standing engagement with feminism disagree: 'The Personal is Political,' we say, 'the way women and girls are treated in their personal lives is actually a political issue.'[1] We suggest that the increasing focus on sex and sexiness is not so much a matter of personal preference but pressure coming from people and institutions in society with the power to shape the way others think and feel. Unfortunately, our critical voices are often silenced by those with a vested interest in keeping women sexualised and trivialised, commodified and subordinated.

The process by which feminist voices have been silenced is an interesting one.[2] Looking back over the last two decades, one can identify deliberate tactics of misrepresentation designed to make equality between the sexes impossible. This tactic involves the twisting of an original message until it appears to mean something else and, then, the promotion of that false version to the public

---

1   The word 'political' does not always refer to the machinations of political parties. Here I use it to denote power dynamics between individuals and groups of people in society. Feminists call on everyone to have a greater awareness of the power dynamics operating between men and women and between the more powerful and less powerful groups in society.

2   Susan Faludi used the word 'backlash' to describe this process in *Backlash: The Undeclared War Against Women* (1991). See also Marilyn French's *The War Against Women* (1992).

through the media and other powerful institutions as though that was what was originally intended.

In this chapter, I will address the issue of trivialising women's and girls' agency in the sexualisation debate by discussing, first, the widely promoted deception that the Feminist Movement equals the so-called Sexual Revolution. Next I will ask: How did sex, sexiness, sexualisation become the measure of women's worth? And how, increasingly, is this measure also applied to girls? Following that, I will outline what feminist researchers and activists see as the harms that come from the sexualisation of women and girls.

The Feminist Movement and the 'Sexual Revolution' compared

As soon as the contraceptive pill became available in the 1960s[3] and women could enjoy sex with little fear of becoming pregnant, those who sought to profit from exploiting women's sexuality began to confuse this newfound sexual freedom with feminism. The message conveyed to society was that a feminist is a woman who is willing to experiment with sex and to make herself constantly available to men for all kinds of sexual experiences. It didn't matter to those promoting such ideas that they were actually the antithesis of the feminist message, which is, above all, about mutual respect and equality.

To this day, women who speak positively about sex, who endorse pornography and prostitution, or who act in overtly sexual ways in public, are often said to be behaving in 'feminist' ways or assumed to be feminists. Even Australian sex therapist Bettina Arndt who, during the 1970s, was associated with *Forum* magazine (a publication encouraging experimentation with a variety of forms of sex), was dubbed a feminist. How she was given that title is curious since any cursory examination of her writing would lead to a serious questioning of that claim.

---

3   The oral contraceptive pill was approved for use in the USA in 1960 and was available in Australia on January 1, 1961. It took some time before health concerns were discussed in public (see Klein, this volume).

In her latest book, *The Sex Diaries* (2009), Arndt strongly rejects the feminist view that women have the right to say 'no' to sex when they don't want it. Her primary concern is for men and their sexual needs. She says that '[t]he right to say "no" needs to give way to saying "yes" more often…' (Arndt, 2009, p. 12). She suggests women—whose libidos she compares to 'damp wood'—work at getting their heads in the right place in the lead-up to sex (p. 81). She supports the idea that women work at reprogramming their minds (p. 82) by conjuring up enjoyable fantasies while their husbands/partners are having sex with them. And, using the language of the market, Bettina Arndt talks about the need for women to keep up the 'sex supply' (p. 128) even when they are not particularly interested in having sex.

An interesting observation is that there seems to be no requirement at all in Arndt's *Sex Diaries* for men to change their behaviour. Her theory is that, if a man is getting all the sex he needs and wants, he will be happier and may very well begin to 'throw a mop around the kitchen floor or wipe down the benches' (p. 177). The onus is on women alone. If they want better relationships with men, it is up to them to change their attitudes and behaviour in relation to sex. The unfortunate message conveyed to girls by such an arrangement is that it's OK for women to use sex as a way of getting something from a man in return—which is, in fact, the basis of prostitution.

One woman's response to Bettina Arndt's book was expressed recently on a feminist email discussion list:

> So what's so surprising that Arndt is championing sex for the fellas? She was at the forefront of the sexual liberation in Aust in 60s & 70s (remember Forum?) And as every thinking person knows the sexual revolution was all about making sex easier, more frequent & with less responsibility for men. It commodified sex. It hoodwinked women into thinking there was some benefit for them. Sexual liberation and feminism are two quite different

things. Women shouldn't feel guilty for maintaining their autonomy, self-respect and independence. It's our basic right (f-agenda email list, March 1, 2009. Quoted with permission from the author).

In addition to our concern about such a negative focus on individual women's sexual responses, many feminists have fought hard against the pornography and prostitution industries, claiming that they encourage the sexualisation and subordination of women and girls. On the other hand, there are those who call themselves feminists who are doing their best to align feminism with the so-called sexual revolution by claiming that prostitution and pornography are empowering for women. Katherine Albury and Catharine Lumby, in their book (with Alan McKee), *The Porn Report* (2008), reject the feminist view that such practices subordinate women to men. They claim that pornography can be good for women and good for relationships. No doubt, the prostitution and pornography industries which make huge profits out of the exploitation of women, depend on liberal feminists such as Albury and Lumby to give legitimacy to their industries.

The tactic of linking feminism with the sexual revolution achieves two goals: a) to give the impression that a woman who freely accepts the sexualisation of women is a strong, liberated woman; and b) to misrepresent feminism and rob it of any chance of being seen as the powerful social and political movement that it is.

Commenting on the so-called sexual revolution, Carole Moschetti writes (2005, p. 232):

...this supposed revolution ushered in an ideology of sexual liberalism which supported the de-censorship of pornography and a sexual relativism around sexual practice that was harmful to women's interests...The effect of this sexual relativism was to shore up men's right to sexual access to girls and women and make feminist campaigning against sexual exploitation more difficult.

While equating the Feminist Movement with the Sexual Revolution is designed to give legitimacy to those who seek to profit from this connection, feminists working for justice and equality make it clear that the feminist movement as they know it is totally opposed to such de-valuing of women.

Sexualisation: the measure of women's worth

How have sex, sexiness and sexualisation gained such favour in recent years as to be the measure by which women's and girls' worth is judged? While it is not a new phenomenon by any means, there is something different about the way it occurs today and how it impacts on younger and younger girls.

Feminists in the 1960s and 1970s spoke out against the sexual objectification of women in beauty pageants, in the media and in advertising. Robin Morgan writes about her involvement in the 1968 women's demonstration against the Miss America pageant in Atlantic City, New Jersey. One of the reasons she cites for targeting the pageant was that 'it is patently degrading to women (in propagating the Mindless Sex-Object Image)...' (Morgan, 1993, p. 25).

In 1970, Morgan wrote the article 'Goodbye to all that' which has become a classic in feminist literature. There is no doubt that one of the reasons for its popularity has been that it expresses the disappointment so many feminists felt, and still feel today, about the sexist attitudes of some men on the Left (see Bray, this volume). Morgan tells of her decision in 1969 to stop writing for *Rat*, a newspaper of the New Left in New York, because its '...new priorities of rock music coverage, pornographic articles and graphics, and sex-wanted ads...began to clog the pages' (pp. 49–50).

In her article, Morgan records some of the horrendously sexist quotes from men on the Left. One 'brother' was heard to say: 'What the hell, let the chicks do an issue [of the newsletter]; maybe

153

it'll satisfy 'em for a while…' (p. 58). In another setting, a 'brother' wrote 'F★ck your women till they can't stand up' (p. 64). Summing up the feelings of so many feminists who have tried to work with men in socialist or Marxist settings throughout the years, Morgan says: 'We have met the enemy and he's our friend' (p. 58).

The sexualising of women by a society which is dominated by men and which exists predominantly to satisfy men's needs is a rather effective way of trivialising and subordinating women. Second Wave feminists like Robin Morgan were aware that a woman who is treated as a sex object is not someone who will be taken seriously. She is there to be used by men and then dismissed or ignored when she attempts to express an opinion or make a serious statement. Fast-forwarding to Bettina Arndt's writing in 2009, again I ask what messages are we passing on to our girls?

With the aim of achieving justice and equality, feminists fought a fierce battle against pornography and its right to exist as a legally sanctioned industry in the USA. In 1983, Catharine MacKinnon and Andrea Dworkin presented a legal ordinance to the City of Minneapolis which they described as 'a sex equality law, a civil-rights law, a law that says that sexual subordination of women through pictures and words, this sexual traffic in women, violates women's civil rights' (MacKinnon, 1990, p. 9). The ordinance was defeated on the grounds that pornography was a 'freedom of speech' issue. It was argued that those who use pornography (mainly men) have a right to do so in a democracy based on individual freedoms. Commenting on the decision some time later, Andrea Dworkin summed it up by saying '…the constitutional rights of the pornographers…superseded in importance the speech rights of women and children who were shut up by pornography' (Dworkin, in Stark and Whisnant, 2004, p. 137). Men's right to free speech, that is, to have access to pornography, was deemed to be more important than women's right to equality, women's right to be treated with respect.[4]

---

4   For a detailed treatment of the issue of pornography as a free vs fair speech issue, see my forthcoming book, *Unspeakable: A feminist ethic of speech.*

The authors of the Northern Territory Government's Little Children are Sacred report (2007) pointed to pornography as a significant contributing factor in the epidemic of child sexual abuse evident in Aboriginal communities in the Northern Territory at that time (Wise and Anderson, 2007). Commenting on the report in an *On Line Opinion* piece, Melinda Tankard Reist expressed the strong view that '(c)hildren suffering porn-driven sexual abuse should come before sex industry profits' (Tankard Reist, 2007). Sheila Jeffreys, in *The Industrial Vagina: The political economy of the global sex trade* (2009) refers to the harmful effects of pornography expressed in the report (pp. 82–83):

> The report is clear that the effects are harmful, stating that "[t]he daily diet of sexually explicit material has had a major impact, presenting young and adolescent Aboriginals with a view of mainstream sexual practice and behaviour which is jaundiced. It encourages them to act out the fantasies they see on screen or in magazines."
>
> The report also blames pornography for the advent of sexualized behaviour evident in young people and even in young children who act out sexually and aggressively towards each other...The problem had got to the point where in one community "girls did not understand that they had a choice to refuse sex. They accepted that if they walked around at night they were available for sex."

To this day, the right to use pornographic, degrading images of women is upheld by the law. Consequently, the pornography industry has grown exponentially to the point where pornographic images of women have now become commonplace in the media, on billboards and other advertising outlets (see Rosewarne, this volume). Feminists and other concerned women and men who speak out against the growing pornification or sexualisation of our culture are derided and accused of being anti-sex. This, of course, is another misrepresentation. To be against the trivialising and subordinating of women and girls for sexual purposes is not at all the same as being against sex.

How is the sexualisation of women and girls different today from the way it occurred when feminists in the 1960s and 1970s were demonstrating against it? Back then, our focus was on the *objectification* of women. Women were used as sex objects by the advertising industry, the media and in men's magazines. Today, the objectification of women continues—and has been extended to girls—but there is an added dimension. Rosalind Gill from the London School of Economics and Political Science argues that sexual objectification has become sexual *subjectification*. In a blatant misrepresentation of the feminist emphasis on empowerment, those who falsely aligned the Feminist Movement with the Sexual Revolution have been able to sell the message that modern, empowered women are 'choosing' to be sexualised. Gill explains that modern day sexualised images are 'organised around sexual confidence and autonomy,' to give the appearance that it is all happening in response to women's demands. Women want it. We are not passive objects being used by advertisers and the fashion industry. Women are subjects who enjoy the attention. In Gill's words (http://monthlyreview.org/mrzine/gill230509.html):[5]

> …what is novel and striking about contemporary sexualised representations of women in popular culture is that they do not (as in the past) depict women as passive objects but as knowing, active and desiring sexual subjects. We are witnessing, I want to argue, a shift from sexual objectification to sexual subjectification in constructions of femininity in the media and popular culture.

Gill is correct in pointing out that all the ways in which women are sexualised now have a subjective element. Women in pornography must be seen to be 'enjoying' the painful, demeaning acts they are required to participate in. In an interview for an anti-

---

5   This online article by Rosalind Gill was originally published in the journal *Feminist Media Studies* (2003).

porn website, porn actress Sarah-Katherine describes pornography in this way (http://www.oneangrygirl.net/antiporn.html):

> I would say that what's shown is basically—it's not revolutionary, it's not different, it's the same old, same old, it's women in uncomfortable positions pretending they feel good, and what's revolutionary about that? What's liberating about that?

Women appearing in pornographic poses in mainstream advertising, too, are required to look like they're enjoying it. Young women gyrating on a pole or on some old man's lap are required to look happy. Women being groped and violated in prostitution are required to look like they're involved and loving it, to keep the customer coming back. It would seem, then, that subjectification has not replaced objectification, as Gill suggests but, rather, that the appearance of subjectification legitimises a greater, more widespread, objectification.

It must be said that feminists are not opposed to women and girls being sexually attractive, or to women and girls enjoying being admired for their beauty. What we are opposed to is the exploitation that almost always accompanies such practices and to the fact that women's worth is measured in this way.

The harms of sexualisation

Together with other like-minded people, feminists speak out against the increasing sexualisation apparent in our culture today because we see it as doing irreparable harm to girls and boys, to women and men, and to the quality of relationships between the sexes. Some of the more obvious harms are as follows:

It de-values women and girls

When women and women's bodies are sexualised and objectified, it presents girls and women as commodities to be looked at, admired, criticised and available to be bought and sold. This makes equality impossible. When feminists in the 1960s and 1970s began to emphasise the need for the empowerment of women, it was so that there would be a greater chance for equality between the sexes. We hoped that women's newfound confidence and self-assurance would mean that they, like men, would be admired for their intelligence and abilities, and take their place alongside men in discussions of national and international importance. Instead, the focus today is once again on women's bodies and their sexuality—and it starts when they are young girls. In a 2009 article in the *Guardian* newspaper, 'Our culture is infected with porn,' UK journalist Sandrine Levêque wrote:

> Pornified culture sends out a disturbing message that women are always sexually available. It dehumanises women into a sum of body parts, reinforces valuing women primarily for their "sex appeal" and undermines healthy sexual relationships…

Far from women being accepted as equals to men, men are once again invited to trivialise and subordinate them. Sexualisation degrades women and girls and legitimates a relationship between the sexes of domination and subordination.

It creates false expectations

When sexualised images of women and girls are in abundant supply throughout society, it creates false expectations in men and boys. The incidence of rape and gang rape of women is evidence of the fact that many men believe that women are there for the taking. Women are seen to be available and, no matter what they do to women, they are confident that they can act with impunity. The trend among teenage boys, too, reveals a belief that it is acceptable to belittle girls as a source of entertainment. Stories of groups of boys abusing and raping girls are all too frequent with the added dimension of filming the abuse and posting it on the Internet and mobile phones.

Sadly, this creates false expectations in women and girls too.

Trying to live up to the 'standard' a sexualised society sets, many work at being more sexy and more available. They submit to cosmetic surgery to alter their bodies, shave off every hint of body hair, adopt a pornified trend in fashion because it is presented as the only option for women who want to be noticed by men and, then, make themselves available to satisfy the sexual needs of men.[6]

It silences women and girls

A particularly disturbing way in which sexualisation harms women and girls was expressed many years ago by the US poet and theorist, Susan Griffin, in terms of silencing one's real self. She says: 'In the wake of pornographic images, a woman ceases to know herself' (1981/1988, p. 202). Griffin expresses concern about little girls being socialised into a pornographic image of a woman because it means that, from very early in life, a girl will begin to shape herself to fit that image. This is only possible, she says, with a degree of self-deception because the sexualised image is a false image. The self-deception required of women and girls is explained by Griffin in terms of two selves:

> One is a false self, manufactured for appearance' sake and set before an audience. This self is allowed to speak, to act, to express, to live. But the other self, who is the real self, is consigned to silence. She is hidden, denied, eventually forgotten, and even, in some cases, unnamed. Thus the deceiver is in danger of never remembering that she has a real self. The real self continues to experience, to feel, to move through life. But in our minds, we destroy her experience, and thus we lose ourselves.

> In a sexualised society, women and girls are required to live out a "pornographic idea of the female" while

---

6   For a detailed description of the lengths to which the so-called beauty industry goes to ensure that women and girls are dissatisfied with their natural bodies, see Sheila Jeffreys' *Beauty and Misogyny: Harmful Cultural Practices in the West* (2005).

our real selves are "cast back into silence" (Griffin, 1981/1988, p. 202).

It interferes with relationships

The concern about relationships expressed in the *Guardian* article quoted above is a real one. A 'pornified culture' does undermine 'healthy sexual relationships,' mainly because it is false and creates false expectations. Men are in danger of deceiving themselves into believing that all women should look slim and sexy and dress in a provocative way and, while most men know that such a picture of women is a fantasy, many live with the feeling that they might have settled for second best when their girlfriend or wife doesn't fit the 'slutty' look. Similarly, women live with the constant reminder (every time they look in the mirror) that they do not measure up to the impossible (and problematic) standards of beauty and sexiness all around them (see Andrusiak, this volume). As a result, what many women bring to their relationships is a low self-esteem and a lack of confidence in their own bodies, while many men try to 'make do' with a partner who is less than the sexualised 'standard model.' Those women who do try to measure up, live lives that are constricted by uncomfortable clothing, stilettos, diets and cosmetic surgery procedures, and spend a great deal of their time in and out of beauty clinics. Men, on the other hand, are free to be their natural selves and to engage with life as it comes.

Relationships suffer, also, when men insist on experimenting with the kinds of degrading sexual activity they see in pornography or fantasise about when confronted with exploitative pictures of women on billboards and other advertising. If his partner refuses, the relationship suffers because he feels that his desire to 'spice up' the sexual side of the relationship has been rejected. And she feels betrayed that he would even consider asking her to submit to such exploitation. If she agrees, the relationship will still suffer because, at some level, both partners know that what they are doing is not 'real.' Their whole relationship is in danger of becoming make-believe in the way that all pornography and sexualisation is make-believe.

Conclusion

Feminists concerned about the increasing sexualisation of our culture are misrepresented and silenced by those who seek to keep women and girls subordinated and sexually available to men. A sexualised culture trivialises and degrades women and girls and insults those men and boys who take no pleasure in seeing the female sex exploited for sexual purposes. It creates false expectations in both sexes, and undermines the potential for relationships between women and men to be real. It makes equality impossible.

References

Arndt, Bettina (2009) *The Sex Diaries. Why Women Go Off Sex and Other Bedroom Battles.* Melbourne University Press, Melbourne.

Dworkin, Andrea (2002) 'Pornography, prostitution, and a beautiful and tragic recent history' in Christine Stark and Rebecca Whisnant (Eds) *Not For Sale: Feminists Resisting Prostitution and Pornography.* Spinifex Press, North Melbourne. pp. 137–145.

Faludi, Susan (1991) *Backlash: The Undeclared War Against Women.* Chatto & Windus, London.

French, Marilyn (1992) *The War Against Women.* Penguin, London; Hamish Hamilton, London.

Gill, Rosalind (2003) 'From sexual objectification to sexual subjectification: The resexualisation of women's bodies in the media' *Feminist Media Studies* 3 (1) pp. 99–106, http://monthlyreview.org/mrzine/gill230509.html

Griffin, Susan (1981/1988) *Pornography and Silence.* The Women's Press, London (1981); Harper and Row, New York (1988).

Jeffreys, Sheila (2005) *Beauty and Misogyny: Harmful Cultural Practices in the West.* Routledge, London and New York.

Jeffreys, Sheila (2009) *The Industrial Vagina: The Political Economy of the Global Sex Trade.* Routledge, London and New York.

Levêque, Sandrine (2009) 'Our culture is infected with porn' *The Guardian,* London, April 24, http://www.guardian.co.uk/commentisfree/2009/apr/24/porn-object-protest-feminism

MacKinnon, Catharine (1990) 'Liberalism and the death of feminism' in Dorchen Leidholdt and Janice G. Raymond (Eds) *The Sexual Liberals and the Attack on Feminism.* Pergamon, The Athene Series, New York. pp. 3–13.

McKee, Alan, Katherine Albury and Catharine Lumby (2008) *The Porn Report.* Melbourne University Press, Melbourne.

McLellan, Betty. *Unspeakable: A Feminist Ethic of Speech* (forthcoming).

Morgan, Robin (1993) 'Women vs. the Miss America Pageant' in Robin Morgan *The Word of a Woman: Selected Prose 1968-1992.* Virago, London. pp. 21–29.

Morgan, Robin (1993) 'Goodbye to all that' in Robin Morgan *The Word of a Woman: Selected Prose 1968-1992.* Virago, London. pp. 49–69.

Moschetti, Carole (2005) Conjugal wrongs don't make rights: international feminist activism, child marriage and sexual relativism. Unpublished PhD thesis, Faculty of Arts, Political Science, Criminology and Sociology, The University of Melbourne.

Tankard Reist, Melinda (2007) 'An invasion of pornography'. *On Line Opinion,* July 23, http://www.onlineopinion.com.au/view.asp?article=6114

Wild, Rex and Alison Anderson (2007) 'Little Children are Sacred.' Report to the Northern Territory Government, http://www.nt.gov.au/justice/docs/depart/annualreports/dpp_annrep_0607.pdf

How Girlhood Was Trashed and What We Can Do to Get It Back: A Father's View

Steve Biddulph

All sex and no love

Sexuality, when fully allowed to unfold, has many aspects. It merges the sacred, the intimate, the sensual, the emotional, the creative, the funny, the tender and the intense. This should be no surprise to us, after all there are no boundaries in the human organism; everything is permeable. Hormones sing in our brains; our thoughts soften our heart muscles; a touch on our skin sparks memories of innocent joy. We are made whole, although life can break us apart.

Our sexuality is wedded to our heart and our mind. For all its problems, most of us still believe that sex can be a radiant and life-affirming thing. So when we see our children grow into beginning adults—what we now call teenagers—we want them to experience it at its very best. To unfold it in their own time and way, and to suffer no harm.

Parents, and perhaps especially parents of girls, have lots of fears about their daughters' sexual safety and wellbeing. There are plenty of age-old hazards—unintended pregnancy, rape, infection.

163

But also the inner harms—loss of trust, loss of the capacity for love, destruction of self worth, death of spirit.

We know, intuitively, and sometimes from bitter experience of our own, that if you hurt someone's sexuality you hurt their soul. When the soul begins to die, the body follows. And sure enough, among sexually abused young women, addiction, depression, self-harm and suicide have always been endemic. As a therapist treating men and women over thirty years, sexual abuse of a child by someone older became the byword, the thing you waited and watched for, in depressed, self-harming, self-doubting, anxious adults or teens. Sexual abuse was so common, you took your time, made the space ready for them to tell you. And conversely, in the gradual healing of broken trust, the symptoms would slowly recede.

Today though, something new has begun to happen in the culture, reported by parents and counsellors, doctors and psychiatrists. The cluster of symptoms that normally result from sexual abuse—self-loathing, depression, addiction, anxiety and difficulty in being close, are now appearing in millions of girls who have not been sexually abused; girls whose family lives are ordinary and safe. Boys are also affected. Adolescence today is a minefield of mental health problems. This was not always so, it is a new and deeply troubling trend. Just what is going on?

One explanation gaining prominence is that our culture itself has become abusive. Some commentators have actually termed this 'corporate paedophilia' (see Rush, this volume), since its motivation is to gratify shareholders and company profits, and its method is to attack and invade young people's psychic space, making them feel badly about their looks, their worth, their social lives and love lives, as a route to selling them more goods.

Media interests have been quick to defend themselves, and to suggest that concern about sexualisation arises from 'wowserism,' some anti-sex impulse. In my experience, the people most concerned, and most angry with the corporate message, are those most in touch with their sexuality; affectionate and vibrant kinds

How Girlhood Was Trashed and What We Can Do to Get It Back:
A Father's View

of people who want the next generation to inherit this freedom of spirit. They are driven by a wish to nurture and empower the young, so that they may experience all that sex and love have to offer. Above all they want young women to be the agents, not the subjects, of their own sexuality. What is happening in our culture as corporate communication so permeates our lives, might be more accurately termed de-sexualisation, the death of sex, the draining out of all spontaneity, connectedness and meaning. I have lived and studied families in many cultures, tribal and rural, eastern and western. It's my view that we are one of the least sexy cultures ever to inhabit the earth. Robbed of inner meaning, tricked out to sell worthless junk, sex in the western world has become a dying shell.

The young feel this most acutely. The romantic, tentative, and tender feelings of young people would surprise many adults. But these positive and loving qualities can easily be battered, bruised and driven underground, if the culture does not reinforce them. There is little poetry left in the culture thrown at young people. For the boys, conditioned by online porn and compliant but disengaged girls, sex may come to have no more meaning than an ice-cream or a pizza. For many girls sex has become a performance, anxiously overlaid with worry about how does my body look? What sexual tricks does he expect or not expect? How do I compare with all the others he has slept with? Little wonder we have one of the most depressed, anxious and lonely generations of young people ever to inhabit the earth.

The hall of mirrors

Sexuality is the means to exploit teens, but marketing begins much younger than that. The war waged by the advertising media on younger girls works primarily by attacking self-image. Instead of seeing oneself from the inside, and from the thoughtful comments of extended family siblings and friends, girls now live in a world of endless unfavourable comparison with the world's most photogenic women. For 99 per cent of our history, most humans never even saw a mirror. Our world consisted of a few dozen real people. We saw beauty in them, and ourselves, based on their kindness, laughter, warmth and care. Images were almost unknown. Today, we see thousands of images a day of total strangers, dressed, made-up, and photo-shopped to look perfect.

The electronic and print media is now so shockingly pervasive, that it has become 'the third parent' for many children. In most homes, television plays throughout breakfast, much of the day, and late into the night. Kids retreat to their room with magazines, music videos, computer screens, or TVs of their own. Outside, the landscape of the urban and suburban world is little better, a barrage of commercial images and messages.

For a teen or pre-teen girl these messages seem to speak to them personally. The mind's automatic response to certain cues cannot be underestimated. Just recently I waited in a fog-bound airport for three hours. Close to my seat was a collecting box in the shape of a life-sized guide dog. Without exception every small child who came past, despite the noise, movement and sensory overload of an airport concourse, saw the animal, and urged their parents to go over to it. We are all programmed to focus on certain cues, and advertisers identified these long ago. For teens, it is other teens. Adolescence is about finding yourself in reflection with others, it is about comparisons and establishing norms, whether we obey or rebel against those. And increasingly, the media world provides these norms. It is more present, more pervasive, more consistent than friends or family. But its message is airbrushed, modelled, posed and utterly unreal. This, it says, is how to succeed socially, how to have a career, how to be liked, be secure and safe, be loved.

By creating or allowing this barrage, particularly the endless examples of youthful beauty that obsess our culture, we have trapped girls in a terrifying hall of mirrors, surrounding them with distorted images of girlhood, always implicitly critical of their selves, always based on externals. In a piecemeal, cumulative way, this is invading and tarnishing girls' vision of themselves, making it almost impossible to put together a positive and integrated sense of self.

It's not just what is there, but also what is missing from this virtual reality. It's a deeply impoverished world view, there is no reflective space, or self searching about values, little in the way of nuanced relationships, which girls used to devour in books and poetry. In this culture, inner qualities are not even mentioned, let alone valued. Loyalty, patience, tenderness, sacrifice, intelligence, grit, endurance, friendliness, individuality itself, are all ignored in favour of body shape, skin tone, hair, and clothing.

The disappearance of caring adults

The attack on girlhood would be less successful if we had not at the same time removed their main defences. In the last thirty years, as we began flooding girls' senses with these narrow versions of womanhood, we were also dismantling the emotional support system that had previously sustained young girls into womanhood. Aunties, grandmas, older women friends, even mothers themselves, became much less available to nurture and reassure, challenge and inform adolescent girls. These women elders were either too busy, too distant geographically, or too preoccupied with their own lives, to be able to offer their time and affirmation.

This has been a remarkable change, more so for the fact that it has largely gone unnoticed. Girls today spend perhaps one tenth of the time in conversation and company of older women than they would have had even fifty years ago. The peer group does its best to fill this gap, and some of the best and most touching moments among young teens are their attempts to nurture and support each other, but it's haphazard. They are not equipped for such a vital and complex role.

The important place of men has diminished too. Fathers, uncles and grandfathers who ideally provided male affirmation and thoughtful conversation free of sexual pressure, once made it possible for a girl to begin seeing herself as intelligent, interesting, capable, strong and fun to be with, independently of any physical attributes. Men are gradually becoming re-activated in their father-hood, but it's very early days. Most daughters wait in despair. A generation of adult women carry the wounds of this absence.

This then is the double jeopardy of girlhood. If no one is helping a girl to appreciate her inner qualities, and she is bombarded with images of womanhood based merely on appearance, something unbalanced begins to happen. A girl's sense of herself becomes more and more external, more and more visual. How she appears to others becomes everything. This leads to the shocking research findings (cited elsewhere in this book) that most girls today hate their own bodies. What an outstandingly successful assault on the mental health of girl children.

What can be done?

The solutions to a problem as massive and complex as the media's assault on the young have to be multiple and overlapping. Parents have some say, in fact a lot of say, about which media they expose their children to. There is a significant move towards not exposing young children to television at all—it has been clearly linked to developmental difficulties of many kinds, from inability to play well or concentrate well, to obesity, anxiety, sleep problems and so on. Parents being proactive with television—switching on to watch a specific program, then switching off—is a very significant improvement in what children are exposed to. Not watching commercial television at all, or at least very selectively, also makes a large difference. Using DVDs and videos instead of live-to-air TV, if electronic childminding is the only way to survive the pre-dinner hour! Not having TVs in children's or teens' bedrooms is probably the best single protection of their mental health. This has been found to drastically reduce TV viewing in total, not to mention exposure to imagery of either a violent or sexually inappropriate kind, with subsequent impacts on anxiety, aggressiveness, and problems with sleep. Another simple and practical measure is simply not buying girls' magazines, most of which are purely marketing vehicles for make-up, clothes and toys they neither need nor benefit from.

But parental actions can only go so far. And the most vulnerable girls will always be the ones who have inept or disempowered parents. Public and governmental action is essential. Most commentators agree that the self-regulatory system for advertising in Australia has failed. As argued so clearly and well by groups like Young Media Australia and Kids Free 2B Kids (see Gale, this volume), regulation of public advertising and careful boundaries around young people's viewing content, have a very large role to play. Advertising aimed at young people is increasingly being disallowed in progressive European societies, on the legal ground that children do not have the cognitive capacity to defend themselves and advertising aimed at them is therefore deceptive and unethical. No economies have collapsed as a result of not exploiting children, but much useless and wasteful consumption has ceased, and that has to be a good thing.

If we value our young, we need to collectively take better care of them. Their whole capacity to be good and happy human beings will grow in direct proportion to this caring, and their sexual happiness and wholeness will be just one aspect of this.

Finding the Courage to Get Real

Tania Andrusiak

On my hard drive is a folder I've called 'Real Women.' In this folder are hundreds of images of women. Some are celebrities, most are not, but all of them are beautiful and brave because they boldly put themselves before the camera in a culture that derides their size or shape. They're not all bigger women, but they all recognise that they have more to offer than their dress size. These women defy the social messages to stay hidden and out of the cultural gaze because they don't 'fit the mould.'

These women live in a world where discrimination based on what your body looks like is legitimised by an unhealthy obsession with manufactured beauty, and the misguided belief that thinness is synonymous with health. This is the same world I inhabit, where I've been told to lose weight since the age of eight, and where people roll their eyes in disbelief if someone suggests they're happy with their body the way it is.

This is the world in which we're asking our daughters to get real about their bodies. It's a world where from ever-younger ages, girls are not just sexualised and diagnosed with eating disorders, but indoctrinated into consumption-driven lives by cosmetic, diet and fashion industries which demand they reject who they are and what they look like, to instead pursue an 'improved' version of themselves.

The images in my folder sit there to inspire me. It's a place of refuge for the days I feel bad about my body. Because if we're serious about 'getting real,' if we want a world where all women are respected and valued, if we're to present future generations of women with options that truly realise the equality offered by feminism, it's going to take more than letters of protest and bans on advertising. It's going to take more than changing legislation or a market-driven 'Pussycat Doll'-concept of girl power, where merely embracing our inner pole dancer amounts to liberation.

For millions of women hating what they see in the bedroom mirror, or dealing with derogatory remarks in the workplace, or wanting to relax in front of the TV without hundreds of images telling them they're not good enough, real change will require one more thing.

Courage.

Getting real is going to take courage.

It's going to take a collaborative effort to reject a mainstream view that values only one size, one shape, one demure pout. Getting real is about having the courage to embrace a diverse range of body shapes and sizes, instead of tearing each other down. It's about looking to one another as allies to combat the disapproving chorus of voices saying 'hasn't *she* let herself go?'

And like our bodies, courage comes in all shapes and sizes.

Courage is my lovely friend Sarah who defies a lifetime of body image struggles by draping her curvaceous body in vibrant colours and beautiful patterns, refusing to fade away and avoid the attention of others.

Courage is the spunky eleven-year-old girl who told me how advertisers wanted girls like her to feel inadequate without the brands they sold in girls' magazines—and who hated the way they made her feel as if buying these brands would make her loved, rather than lonely, in the school playground.

Courage is the women of size whose blogs I read; women who refuse to buckle under degrading comments made by ill-informed health professionals. Courage is the women who go for health checks even when they fear being lectured or ridiculed about their weight. Or who gather courage to attend appointments for their annual Pap smear and insist on having it even when they are told to come back when they've lost weight.

Courage is also a Melbourne GP who, with his fabulous 2004 book, *If Not Dieting, Then What?*, provides a desperately-needed antidote to the body hatred gripping our culture. Since meeting the author, Rick Kausman, we've shared ideas and stories about body image, the diet industry and its impact on so many lives—particularly women—but also their partners, families and communities.

It was through Rick that I found myself sharing teenage stories with Jeri.

Jeri has spent a lifetime dealing with anorexia, having been hospitalised several times to stabilise her weight. Now supporting her ageing parents, every day Jeri summons the courage to swim— an activity she described to me as a 'passion for being enveloped in water'—knowing that her love for swimming is only matched by her hatred of exposing her body in public. She keeps on going, even when people tell her, with no hint of irony, that they'd kill to have a body like hers.

Rick noted that we often hear of courage in the context of men and sporting achievements. But when, he asked, do we celebrate the courage of women who struggle to live normal lives with deeply ingrained body image issues? When do we celebrate women like Jeri, whose actions are completely normal, yet incredibly brave?

Jeri's quiet courage may go unrecognised. But it is rich in her caring for her parents and her refusal to give up swimming, no matter how confronting it may be. More than that, courage resonates in her ability to just keep going in a culture that too often glamourises her isolating and debilitating illness. It is there in her simple desire to share painful stories with me: to connect with someone she didn't even know.

As we talked, Jeri and I managed to laugh about our similar food and weight obsessions; mine due to bulimia, hers through anorexia. I couldn't believe she beat me at obsessive weighing: my 'scales-in-a-day' personal record was 30. But Jeri tells me she'd step on them a hundred times a day. A hundred times. Just getting on, getting off, and getting on again.

What were we looking for? A magic number? Permission to actually like ourselves? Happiness? Who knows. But we both knew how it felt to look in the mirror and utterly *hate* what we saw. Who am I? *That* ghastly reflection? Ugh. What a disappointment. It's called the hate train, girls. Catch it at your nearest newsagent.

But we don't just find it there. It's so often handed to us as we first catch our mothers looking in the mirror at their own bodies with disgust. It's there on the covers of women's magazines that tower over us at supermarket registers. Young girls learn about it in every ad, TV show, Disney movie and music video they see.

Most young women understand only too well that obsessing over weight and appearance is simply expected of them. And why wouldn't it be, when maintaining a 'perfect' body defines so many of the role models we're expected to admire? When women's bodies are now expected to snap back like elastic bands as soon as we've given birth? How do we fight against a mindset this immense, this entrenched?

Waging our own war against the magazines, building-sized billboards and ignorant comments from family and friends takes courage. Ignoring the calls to be skinnier, prettier, sexier, to eat less, spend more time at the gym, to count calories everyday of our lives takes courage too.

And while it's hard to reject the ideals of flawless beauty and a size zero body, it's much more painful to *not* fight it. In pursuing the 'body beautiful,' we commit to looking in the mirror and wishing we were different. We undervalue the gifts and talents that make us who we really are. We reject the truth that women are perfect *without* the constant dieting, waxing, buying and dyeing.

This is the price we pay when we buy into the beauty myth: in looking so hard at the fake images before us, we never get to see how much stronger we'd all be if we looked to each other instead. Our culture's obsession with the 'perfect body' creates a distance between us.

Even worse, it leaves us with fewer ways to really connect. It pushes us to unite through games that prove our own body hatred: games like 'my thighs are bigger than yours' keep us from understanding one another. They prevent us from hearing each others' stories. And, like Jeri and I, from hearing just how similar we really are.

If we looked to each other instead of the digital mannequins in front of us, we could find the courage to show our children and communities what it means to get real. We could stop making apologies for the bodies we find ourselves in: 'Oh, my bum's too big. My breasts are too small.'

But, too big for what? Too small for whom? If we don't ask these questions, we forget the impossible standard we're comparing our bodies against: a fantasy designed not to give birth, or age, or embrace the cyclical nature of life, but one designed to sell product, titillate men and give us a goal so unachievable that we will never stop spending. Some role model.

This is the final result of a culture so allergic to body diversity: it isolates us from our own bodies. It makes a series of problems out of every one of us: problems that only consumption can solve. Bodies designed to nurture life are reduced to the sum of their parts. Our worth is based on our ability to fit a physical mould representing less than three per cent of the population.

So here's the real bottom line: this epidemic of body hatred makes a few select people very rich; and so many of us very sad.

175

Who decided that a body isn't 'good enough' until its excess fat is shed and its loose skin pruned, or stretched, or pinned back? What would happen if every mother found the courage to love her own body, so that her children may learn to love theirs?

What if we found the courage to talk back to ads, or refuse to take the number on the bathroom scales as an indication of our worth? What if we found the courage to get out and move our bodies simply because it *feels* good, not because we want to be three sizes smaller?

What if we *all* started collecting images of real women in their myriad shapes and sizes, and began to see a more accurate picture of true body diversity? Would we begin to see that what's reflected back at us in celebrity images and advertisements isn't normal?

Would we instead find the courage to look back at our own genetic heritage and realise that our bodies mirror those of our relatives and ancestors? Could we look to the bodies of real women our own age? Because if we did, we'd see breasts of all different shapes and sizes. We'd see drooping tummies and generous bottoms; uneven nipples and stretch marks. We'd see floppy underarms and inner thighs, and dimpled flesh on even the thinnest of bodies. All normal. All perfect for the bodies they find themselves on.

Or what if we organised to meet in groups small and large, in cities and the most remote of rural places, to raise our voices against the media manipulation of women's bodies and to call for greater diversity in media representations of women? We could call ourselves Women Unite (or something fabulous!) and use it to connect, like Jeri and I, by sharing stories and finding comfort in our similar struggles.

If we worked at it, eventually it would serve its purpose. Then we could return to our tennis clubs, barbecues, environmental groups or belly dancing classes—or even just to Saturday nights with friends—and talk about something other than how women look, who's had botox, and how much weight we've lost or gained. How great would it be if, instead of greeting each other with, 'Wow, have you lost weight?' we said, 'Wow! You've learnt something new!'

Or what if we simply started by asking ourselves what the deal is with this obsession with women's bodies? Aren't we sick of the amount of attention paid to those who pass or fail the perfection ideal? Who cares if Britney Spears has gained four pounds? Why on earth is it breaking news if an actor has bumpy thighs? Don't we all?

We urgently need to find the courage to see through these images.

Because the women we're dying to emulate are nothing more than collaborative works of persuasive art, manufactured by teams of creative people, driven to synthesise and execute an idea for sale. They are not prescriptions or directions for a happy life.

And the truth is that no, pictures of thin women alone won't *give* you an eating disorder. But they will certainly increase the possibility of one. Trust me: these images will rule your life if you let them. They'll steal your brain. They'll poke holes in your self-confidence. They'll drive you to harm your bodies in ways you can't imagine.

These images don't just say, 'Here, buy our product.' They say, 'Here. Buy our dream.' But it's an empty jar. The emperor has no clothes.

Look. All of us bleed. We all sweat, fart, burp and smell more like one another than any of us would care to imagine. We all dance, cry, dream, sing and want to rip our hearts out when someone we love dies. That's because we're all human. All of us.

Each of us is an exquisite symphony of muscles, nerves and synapses. Our bodies are extraordinary vehicles given to us to experience this earth, our lives. Yes, our bellies sag, our breasts droop and our skin crumples as we age. It's inescapable. Our bodies will change with time. It takes courage to accept the inevitable cycles of life. We can't keep back the tide forever.

And, why would you want to?

References

Kausman, Rick (2004) *If Not Dieting, Then What?* Allen & Unwin, Sydney.

One Woman's Activism: Refusing to Be Silent

Julie Gale

In 2005, I was thinking about a theme for my next one-woman show at the Melbourne International Comedy Festival. I explored what was annoying me most—this is always a good starting point and I love satire. It was clear that I was becoming increasingly angry about what my young children were exposed to. Sexualised imagery on outdoor advertising, sexualised dolls, sexualised lyrics on CDs marketed to little girls and highly sexualised music video clips in kids' viewing times on TV to name a few. Over the next two years I talked with many parents, collected personal anecdotes and began to formulate ideas for the show. I became aware that while most parents expressed concerns, they felt powerless to change anything. Others were reluctant to express concern at all, in case they'd be labelled 'prudes.'

A billboard appeared at the end of my street which read 'SEX FOR LIFE.' I stood there looking at it thinking 'what the…?' Do my kids really need to be reading this on the way to the park? What a conversation starter! 'What's sex for life, mum?' 'Well, darling, it's about all those men out there who can't get it up anymore.' Yeah right! This billboard was eventually

replaced with 'For a Star Performance…Premature Ejaculation and Erection Problems.' The text itself was graphic enough, but the 'woman' featured in the ad looked about fourteen-years-old.

I was angry that my kids were involuntarily forced to ask questions about male sexual dysfunction before they had even a chance to ask about their own naturally emerging sexuality. This time I thought, 'you guys have picked the wrong street!'

Around the same time The Australia Institute released its Corporate Paedophilia report (see Rush, this volume). The report said there had been 'no sustained public debate' about the issue in Australia. So I scrapped the one-woman show and started raising awareness.

I formed Kids Free 2B Kids (KF2BK) in February 2007 and set up an alliance with Young Media Australia (now the Australian Council on Children and the Media).

I was contacted by journalist Deborah Gough who had heard about my idea to organise a meeting between child development experts and politicians in Canberra. The following week an article about KF2BK and an image of the 'Premature Ejaculation' billboard appeared in The Sunday Age (Gough, 2007a). I was taken by surprise to be contacted by so many people—both in Australia and internationally—who were eager to voice concerns and share personal stories. A segment about the campaign aired on Today Tonight (March 29, 2007) and after that I was literally inundated. And, strike one: the premature ejaculation billboard disappeared!

The Sunday Age ran a series of articles over the following weeks which really helped to move the debate along. The Australian Association of National Advertisers (AANA) announced it would review the advertising to children codes.[1]

---

1 'Sexual imagery in advertising may be toned down following a Melbourne mother's campaign for higher standards. The Australia Association of National Advertisers, which sets the ethical codes for advertising, said it was concerned about the public outcry against the sexualisation of children in advertising. The association's executive officer, Collin Segelov, said the subject had been raised this week by its board at an industry meeting. Mr Segelov said it was a direct result of the Kids Free 2B Kids campaign led by Elsternwick mother Julie Gale, which was first revealed in The Sunday Age' (Gough, 2007b, p. 5).

In the early days of the campaign, there was opposition from a couple of media academics who were adamant that the sexualisation of children was not an issue. Any concerns voiced were condescendingly dismissed as 'moral panic.' Similarly, certain advertisers suggested that people who had a problem with sexualised imagery on billboards were 'a very small minority who are uncomfortable discussing the subject of sex with their children.'[2]

It was obvious to me from the start that many of these opposing views focussed on adults. For example, parents who can't talk about sex with their children, parents who are prudes or wowsers, parents who are religious, or adults who don't have a sense of humour. A common and tiresome excuse from the advertising industry is that ads are 'humorous and irreverent' and that the 'target audience' gets it—what they don't say is 'bugger the rest of you!' While a minority of parents may fall into the above categories, in my experience most do not.

The term 'moral panic' is tiresome, lazy and predictable (see Bray, this volume). It's used as a put-down to people with differing views and is an excuse not to engage in the real issues. I find it amusing that this assumption has often been made of me. Along the way I've been called a 'crusader' and a 'self-appointed moral guardian.' According to one critic, I've 'let loose a kind of hysteria in Australian society' with 'something between gusto and zealotry.' Apparently I'm also a 'booster of populist politicians' and have 'entirely predictable tut-tutting' (Fine, 2008). Hilarious!

Growing up in a small country town in the 1970s meant I experienced how a 'community' works, where people tend to care about each other and their environment. I've also lived in the city for over twenty years, and see how that sense of 'community' is lost. That's one way the marketing and advertising machine gets its power. In the city we don't seem to have a sense of ownership

---

2 Advertising Standards Board. Case report complaint reference number 20/07: 'Overall the greater good served by such a message should prevail over the discomfort felt by a very small minority who are uncomfortable discussing the subject of sex with their children.' http://www.advertisingstandardsbureau.com.au/pages/index.asp

about our surroundings. We pass a giant billboard depicting a sexually objectified woman, or words like 'Want Longer Lasting Sex?' and we keep driving. We mightn't like it, but we shrug our shoulders and think 'well, what can I do about it?'

The Advertising Standards Board (ASB) relies on people making complaints. Most people don't realise that billboards are not screened or vetted before they go out into the public arena, and action will only take place if complaints are received (see Rosewarne, this volume).

Speaking up and making complaints has helped to instigate a lot of change since forming KF2BK, and the issue has received extensive media exposure:

- The Senate Inquiry into the Sexualisation of Children in the contemporary media environment (June 2008) and changes to the advertising codes for children (April 16, 2008) have been positive steps forward (http://www.aana.com.au/documents/CodeChildren.pdf);
- Holeproof and Target withdrew sexualised underwear aimed at young girls (http://www.aph.gov.au/Senate/committee/eca_ctte/sexualisation_of_children/responses/target1.pdf) (Critchley, 2007a and b; Danaher, 2007);
- Bras N things reconsidered how they were displaying 'adult-only' products in their outlets (http://www.aph.gov.au/Senate/committee/eca_ctte/sexualisation_of_children/responses/brasnthings.pdf);
- The ASB determined that the Advanced Medical Institute (AMI) had breached section 2 of the advertisers code of ethics. AMI subsequently removed its 'Want Longer Lasting Sex?' billboards (http://www.adstandards.com.au/pages/index.asp (Complaint Ref 278/08 August 2008)[3] (http://www.abc.net.

3   The AMI still don't get it though. The latest attempts at wooing men with erection problems to purchase their products have been billboards stating: 'Men "DO IT" longer and Bonk Longer.' 'Shonk' longer more like it—the 'Doctor' who owns the company is not registered in Australia and none of AMI's products are registered with the Therapeutic Goods Administration (TGA).

au/news/stories/2008/08/26/2346336.htm);[4]

- *Girlfriend* magazine stopped advertising *Playboy* products after I told them they were effectively grooming young girls to wear the major brand of the pornography industry. The marketing manager I spoke with didn't seem to understand the problem. She sighed and told me that there was 'no logo on the T-shirt.' So I said 'Mmm, the text says *Playboy* is a collection of clothing and swimwear for the trendy savvy fashionable girl. Cute and Innocent—cool and tough all at the same time. *Playboy* is one brand you should include in your wardrobe—and you're telling me that you are giving away free *Playboy* T-shirts that don't have the logo on it? Now that's very curious.' She then admitted that she hadn't actually seen them. I didn't hear back from her and only found out about the outcome when I read *Girlfriend's* response in submissions to the Senate Inquiry (2008, p. 5.) (http://www.aph.gov.au/Senate/committee/eca_ctte/sexualisation_of_children/submissions/sub130.pdf);
- *Dolly* and *Girlfriend* magazines have stopped advertising mobile phone wallpapers which say, for example, 'I'm a good girl dressed in the body of a slut.' Or: 'Sex when it's good it's really good, when it's bad it's still pretty good,' 'Save a virgin, do me instead' and 'Free Sex Just Ask.' Magazines for young girls are not regulated, so it is very important to know what our daughters are reading;
- Jay Jay's removed its 'Little Losers' range of T-shirts after community outcry. The logos read 'Mr Asshole,' 'Mr Agro,' 'Mr Drunk,' 'Mr Pimp,' 'Mr Well-Hung,' 'Miss Bitch,' 'Miss Floozy,' and 'Miss Wasted.' Given Jay Jay's supports *Reachout* which provides assistance to kids and young teens dealing with issues such as mental health and body image, sex, drugs

---

4   In February 2009, the UK Advertising Standards Authority (ASA) ordered the AMI 'Want Longer Lasting Sex?' advertisement down because it breached the Responsible Advertising and Decency codes. It also concluded that the AMI had indirectly advertised an unlicensed medicine and also breached the medicines code http://www.asa.org.uk/asa/adjudications/Public/TF_ADJ_45797.htm

and alcohol abuse, perhaps it recognised the contradiction (Brooks, 2008; Kohler, 2008);

- The 'What's New' chain in family shopping malls sold blow-up sex dolls alongside Wiggles merchandise. So I decided to email the Wiggles corporation to ask if they were comfortable selling their Dorothy-the-dinosaur mugs on a shelf opposite a 'Granny I'd like to F*ck' blow-up doll. They withdrew their merchandise the same day from all 'What's New' stores (author e-mail correspondence, June 11, 2008);

- Smiggle withdrew its Voodoo Doll pencil case—which was sold with a photo slot and real pins—when KF2BK and child development professionals spoke out about the potential for bullying. An article appeared in *The Herald Sun* (Critchley, 2009), and I was contacted by many parents. One mother had already attempted to get a response from the company after explaining that her thirteen-year-old daughter had been bullied using the voodoo doll with her face on it (see Tankard Reist, 2009);

- BP, Shell-Coles Express and Mobil withdrew all Category 1 pornographic magazines from their company-owned stores nationwide (author correspondence with Coles and BP, November 2008, and telephone conversation with Mobil, December 2008);

- In May 2009, moments before submitting this chapter, documents obtained by KF2BK under Freedom of Information laws confirmed that retailer David Jones used advertisements intending to sexualise children as young as ten. The documents from the New South Wales Office of the Children's Guardian revealed information indicating that young girls aged ten to twelve years be posed 'slightly more adult and sexy.'

Although not made known through the FOI documents, according to the *Daily Telegraph* (Fife-Jeomans, 2009), a freelance photographer working for advertising agency Saatchi & Saatchi told the Children's Guardian the campaign was meant to be a bit provocative. 'The age is from ten to twelve years so slightly more adult and sexy,' the photographer said, according to the report.

KF2BK called on David Jones to issue apologies to the children, their parents and the Australia Institute (see Rush, this volume, whose original allegations against David Jones are now vindicated; KF2BK, 2009; Black, 2009 and Hamilton, 2009).

But of course the battle against irresponsible corporations continues. I have also been involved in a campaign against Unilever. In response to letters from KF2BK and the Campaign for a Commercial Free Childhood in the United States, Unilever issued a global statement acknowledging the contradiction between its highly sexualised *Lynx/Axe* advertising and the *Dove* self-esteem programs for young girls. Unilever owns both companies. Predictably though, their statement was full of the 'humorous' and 'target market' spiel. More work needs to be done to address the extraordinary hypocrisy of this company and others like it.

I believe that the *Dove* self-esteem programs are cynical marketing ploys to get product placement into young girls' lives as early as possible. If Unilever cared at all about women and girls, they wouldn't be teaching young males that women are sexual predators and sexually available anytime; they wouldn't be co-marketing with *Playboy*; and they certainly wouldn't be selling the message to Indian and Asian women that to get ahead in life and love you need to whiten your skin. *Fair and lovely* is a skin whitening cream and in India, Unilever has set up the *Fair and Lovely Foundation*. Hypocritically, their mission statement is 'Empowering women in India to change their destinies through education, career guidance and skills training.' Woops, they forgot to say 'but girls, you'd better whiten up first!' The *Dove* 'Real Women' campaign?—oh puhlease![5]

---

5   An article in *The New Yorker* in May 2008 contained the interesting admission by the world's most famous airbrush artist Pascal Dangin, that he touched up the images of the 'real women' in the Dove 'Real Beauty' campaign. Journalist Lauren Collins writes: 'I mentioned the Dove ad campaign that proudly featured lumpier-than-usual "real women" in their undergarments. It turned out it was a Dangin job. "Do you know how much retouching was on that?" he asked. "But it was great to do, a challenge, to keep everyone's skin and faces showing the mileage but not looking unattractive"' (Collins, 2008).

I have an ongoing issue with stores in family shopping centres that sell ostensibly to children, but display R-rated merchandise within children's easy access and view.

In the Senate Inquiry, I presented examples of merchandise, including blow-up sex dolls, sold in the 'What's New' chain and was asked to make an official complaint to the police. Unfortunately, the complaint could not be processed because there are currently no laws protecting children from this involuntary exposure. I spoke with centre management at the Chadstone Shopping Centre in Melbourne, and the response was 'well don't go into the shop if you're offended by it.' I explained that the issue isn't whether I (or any adult) am offended; the issue is the impact on children. No action was taken and 'What's New' has ignored correspondence from KF2BK.

In 'What's New,' children can view a game called 'Let's F★CK' or flick through 'Triple X Vouchers' complete with images of a 'Tit-F★cking Session,' a 'Blow Job' and a mutual 'Masturbation Session.' The text on the box of a blow-up doll says '3 Love holes for your pleasure—Oral, Vaginal or Anal.' Not quite what you'd expect in a store that sells Beanie kids, fairies and teddies! Commendations to the Wiggles for getting their products out of these stores. It's not rocket science to work out that children's and 'adult-only' merchandise do not belong on the same premises.

In late 2008, I was in a milk bar buying an ice-cream with my ten-year-old son. On the same shelf as the daily newspapers and women's magazines was a porn magazine titled 'Live Young Girls—Tender Teenage Twat.' The top third of the magazine was visible and displayed a young looking female wearing pigtails. I thought 'how can this possibly be legal?' I decided to investigate further and found that teen porn magazines are very common in convenience stores, newsagents, milk bars and petrol stations. I bought a selection so I could photograph the titles and check the content.

The magazines were classified Category 1. This means they are not allowed to depict anyone who is under eighteen or who 'appears' to be under eighteen. They are also not permitted to depict graphic sex acts. Category 1 classified magazines are allowed to be sold in the public arena if they are sealed.

I looked up the classification guidelines and, surprisingly, discovered that almost 100 per cent of the magazines I had purchased were illegal. An audit by the Australian Classification Board validated my findings (author correspondence with Donald McDonald, Director, Classification Board, December 16, 2008; Davies, 2009).

Much of the text in these magazines implies sex with minors. The images are full of young looking girls wearing school uniforms, pink headbands, pigtails and braces on their teeth. They are often posed surrounded by soft toys. Most would be given an RC—that is a 'refused classification'—by the Classification Board because they breach the guidelines. This means they should not even be sold in an adult-only venue. Many distributors are flouting the law by sealing illegal magazines with official Category 1 labels and selling them to retailers.

The following are examples of highly visible text on front covers of teen porn magazines which are frequently on shelves next to 'teen' magazines like *Dolly* and *Girlfriend.*

Cum on my Braces—Virgin Babe

Petite—Young Girls Eager for Anal

F*ckable Flatties Special

Slumber Party Sluts—Our filthiest issue ever. 12 Tight Twats

Back To School Special

Pigtailed School Girl—'My first 3-way'

Spunky Teen Sluts

Cum Hungry Virgins Inside

Awkward Teen Sluts—Amateurs

Young Girls Getting Laid

Teen Porn Star Collectors Issue

We already face the problem that Internet porn provides easy access and anonymity to those who want it. But allowing pornography that incites sex with minors to be sold in the public arena is openly validating abhorrent behaviour. I talked about the issue on radio and it was also raised in Senate Estimates hearings in October 2008 and May 2009 (*Hansard*, 2008, pp. 111–113, 120; *Hansard,* 2009, pp. 57–66).

One way of getting action throughout the KF2BK campaign has been to photograph inappropriate merchandise, advertising or content in publications and email it to executives and CEOs. It's important they know what their companies are selling!

That's how we got BP, Shell-Coles Express and Mobil to withdraw all Category 1 pornographic magazines from their company-owned stores nationwide (author correspondence with Coles and BP, November 2008, and telephone conversation with Mobil, December 2008).

7-Eleven chose to ignore the information. A representative told me she was sure their 'family friendly' stores would not stock such magazines. They do, and I provided the evidence—but still no action (author emails and phone contact with 7-Eleven, December 2008). Others, such as Caltex/Safeway abdicated all responsibility to their franchisees (author telephone contact, December 2008). United Petroleum and McDonalds, which co-brand with Fuelzone, have ignored all correspondence (e-mails and telephone contact, December 2008). It was difficult to get media coverage about this issue as, ironically, the magazine titles (which are on public display) are deemed inappropriate to print or show on TV! New South Wales Labor MP Greg Donnelly made a speech about the magazines in parliament and was told by Opposition Leader Barry O'Farrell that he had 'gone well beyond the bounds of good taste and common sense' for reading out the titles.

A *Daily Telegraph* report described Mr Donnelly's actions as bizarre (in Benson, 2009). If it's bad taste to read them out in parliament, then why should the rest of the community, particularly children, be subjected to them?

I sent 28 teen porn magazines to the Classification Board and asserted they were illegal. Director Donald McDonald agreed that all 28 magazines failed to comply with Category 1 guidelines. Eleven were refused classification (RC),[6] thirteen were unclassified,[7] and four were Category 2, which should have been limited to adult-only venues. None of the distributors complied with the Board's 'please explain' notices and law enforcements were notified (author correspondence with Donald McDonald, Director, Classification Board, December 16, 2008).[8]

Julie-Anne Davies wrote a piece in *The Australian* detailing the teen porn magazine issue and the failure of the Classification Board to do its job (Davies, 2009). Classification Board Deputy Director, Olya Booyar, said 'enforcement of current laws was heavily reliant on public complaints. The public is not as forthcoming as it could be and we cannot be everywhere.' Until I read this statement I had no idea that our classification system relied on public complaints. I assumed that the state and territory police enforced the Guidelines. They are supposed to! It took one persistent voice to get this issue raised—imagine the change we could create if more of us acted. This is about illegal magazines that incite sex with minors being sold in the public arena. A classification system that allows this is an utter failure.

---

6   Publications which fall within the criteria for 'RC' cannot be legally imported or sold in Australia (Australian Classification Board *Guidelines for the Classification of Publications* 2005, p. 14).

7   Publications which have not been presented to the board for classification are deemed 'Unclassified.'

8   EROS, which represents the sex industry in Australia, claims to care about child protection. Yet its secretary, David Watt, imports some of the worst teen porn magazines mentioned in this piece. Watt is named variously as General Manager of Namda (the company name under which applications to the Classification Board were made) and Windsor Wholesale. The titles imported by Namda/Windsor are in milk bars, supermarkets and petrol stations (see Tankard Reist, 2008).

I have been asked to give presentations on many occasions, both in Australia and overseas. A particular highlight was being invited by The Hon. Alistair Nicholson, former Chief Justice of the Family Court, to speak at an international conference on Child Labour and Child Exploitation in Cairns in August 2008. I saw this as a powerful acknowledgement of the shift that has occurred since I started the campaign. The sexualisation of children is beginning to be recognised in the context it deserves: child exploitation.

KF2BK acts as a conduit for the community to express concerns. People should not underestimate the power of their own voices. I encourage everyone to register their names onto our website www.kf2bk.com as a way of being heard. There's definitely power in numbers, and speaking up really does make a difference!

I have a quote on my office wall that I refer to often.

'To avoid criticism, do nothing, say nothing, be nothing.'
Elbert Hubbard

As long as we stay silent, we are complicit in maintaining the status quo.

References

Australian Government (2005) 'Guidelines for the Classification of Publications' http://www.comlaw.gov.au/comlaw/management.nsf/lookupindexpagesbyid/IP200508204?OpenDocument

Australian Government (2008) 'Senate Inquiry into the sexualisation of children in the contemporary media environment' accessed June, http://www.aph.gov.au/SENATE/committee/eca_ctte/sexualisation_of_children/report/report.pdf

Benson, Simon (2009) 'MP Greg Donnelly outrages parliament with adult titles' *The Daily Telegraph,* Sydney, March 27, http://www.news.com.au/dailytelegraph/story/0,27574,25247801-5006009,00.html

Black, Sophie (2009) 'FOI reveals DJs kids were supposed to be "adult and sexy"' accessed June 1, http://www.crikey.com.au/2009/06/01/foi-reveals-djs-kids-were-supposed-to-be-adult-and-s-xy/

Brooks, Karen (2008) 'Shirty with little misses' *Courier Mail,* January 23, http://www.news.com.au/couriermail/story/0,23739,23091541-5012471,00.html

Collins, Lauren (2008) 'Pixel perfect: Pascal Dangin's virtual reality' *The New Yorker,* May 12, http://www.newyorkerest.com/?p=36

Critchley, Cheryl (2007a) 'Kylie gets her knickers knotted' *The Herald Sun*, June 15.

Critchley, Cheryl (2007b) 'Little Kylie syndrome' *The Herald Sun,* June 16.

Critchley, Cheryl (2009) 'Voodoo Smiggle furore' *The Herald Sun*, March 18, p. 23.

Danaher, Carla (2007) 'Racy wear for kids under fire' *The Herald Sun,* June 16.

Davies, Julie-Anne (2009) 'Underage porn sold in corner milkbars' *The Australian*, April 3, p. 5.

Fine, Duncan (2008) 'Bill Henson? Porn culture? Get real' accessed May 30, http://www.crikey.com.au/2008/05/30/bill-henson-porn-culture-get-real

Fife-Yeomans, Janet (2009) 'Row brews over children's "sexy" David Jones ad' accessed May 30, http://www.news.com.au/dailytelegraph/story/0,22049,25558480-5001021,00.html

Gough, Deborah (2007a) 'Innocence interrupted: move to end selling sex to children' *The Sunday Age*, Melbourne, March 25.

Gough, Deborah (2007b) 'Advertisers heed outcry over sex and kids' *The Sunday Age*, Melbourne, April 8, p. 5.

Hamilton, Clive (2009) 'DJs & Saatchi approved sexed-up kids. So why come after us?' accessed June 2, http://www.crikey.com.au/2009/06/02/clive-hamilton-djs-saatchi-approved-sxed-up-kids-so-why-come-after-us/

Hansard (2008) Senate, Standing Committee on Legal and Constitutional Affairs of the Senate, October 20, pp. 111–113, 120, http://www.aph.gov.au/hansard/senate/commttee/S11351.pdf

Hansard (2009) Legal and Constitutional Legislation Committee, May 25, pp. 57–66, http://www.aph.gov.au/hansard/senate/commttee/S12039.pdf

Kids Free 2B Kids (2009a) 'David Jones sprung for ads sexualising children,' May 31, Media Release http://www.kf2bk.com/latest_news.htm&news_id=15

Kohler, Chris (2008) 'Jay Jays reaches out to losers everywhere' accessed January 24, http://www.crikey.com.au/2008/01/24/jay-jays-reaches-out-to-losers-everywhere

Tankard Reist, Melinda (2008) 'Incensed about censorship' accessed November 27, http://www.abc.net.au/unleashed/stories/s2429316.htm

Tankard Reist, Melinda (2009) ' Sticks and stones, pins and needles' accessed March 24, http://www.abc.net.au/unleashed/stories/s2521872.htm

CONTRIBUTORS

Tania Andrusiak is a 35-year-old writer, editor and mother of two. She has written and edited content for commercial and non-profit sectors including Oxfam Australia, *Eureka Street*, *On Line Opinion* and *MercatorNet*. She is the co-author of a book on parenting and media literacy, *Adproofing Your Kids* (Finch Publishing, 2009).

Steve Biddulph's books on parenthood are in four million homes and in 29 languages worldwide. He has been a psychologist for 30 years. Steve recently led a five-year national project to remember the 353 parents and children who died on the refugee vessel SIEVX, at the height of the 2001 federal election. (www.sievxmemorial.com) He lives among a large extended family in Tasmania.

Dr Abigail Bray is a post-doctoral research fellow at the University of Western Australia. She has published on anorexia nervosa, the psychiatric drugging of children, and child sexual abuse 'moral panics' in international refereed journals. She is the author of *Helene Cixous: Writing and Sexual Difference* (2004) and *Body Talk: A Power Guide for Girls* (2005) with Elizabeth Reid Boyd. She is a member of the Marxist collective 'Das Argument: Journal for philosophy and social sciences.'

Selena Ewing is a founding director of Women's Forum Australia, and Senior Research Officer at Southern Cross Bioethics Institute, Adelaide. Selena has a background in health science and her research interests include women's health, aged care and public health. She is the author of *Women and Abortion: An Evidence-Based Review* and *Faking It: The Female Image in Young Women's Magazines*.

Dr Melissa Farley is a feminist psychologist. In 2003, she edited *Prostitution, Trafficking & Traumatic Stress* (Routledge) and in 2007 she wrote *Prostitution and Trafficking in Nevada: Making the Connections* (Prostitution Research & Education). Melissa Farley is director of Prostitution Research & Education, a nonprofit organization based in San Francisco (http://www.prostitutionresearch.com) and she is a founding member of the Nevada Coalition Against Sex Trafficking (nevadacoalition.org).

Julie Gale is a comedy writer and performer and the founder of Kids Free 2B Kids (www.kf2bk.com). She has performed her one-woman shows at the Melbourne International Comedy Festival. Julie has been raising public, corporate and political awareness about the sexualisation of children since February 2007.

Professor Clive Hamilton AM is Charles Sturt Professor of Public Ethics at the Centre for Applied Philosophy and Public Ethics, based at the Australian National University. For fourteen years until early 2008 he was the Executive Director of The Australia Institute. He is the author of *Growth Fetish* and *The Freedom Paradox*, both published in Australia by Allen & Unwin.

Author and publisher **Maggie Hamilton** gives frequent talks and lectures, is a regular media commentator and a keen observer of social trends. Her book *What Men Don't Talk About*, about the lives of real men and boys, has been published in Australia, New Zealand, Holland, the Arab States and Brazil. Her most recent book is *What's Happening To Our Girls?* (2008) Maggie is currently researching *What's Happening To Our Boys?* to be published mid-2010.

Noni Hazlehurst OA is one of Australia's most distinguished and respected actors in film and television. The recipient of four AFI Awards and two Logies, Noni has worked extensively in theatre in Australia and overseas. She has been a performer and writer for *Playschool* for 24 years and both patron and ambassador for a number of child welfare organisations, such as Barnardos. A regular presenter for ABC radio, a frequent contributor to newspapers and magazines on issues of child protection and parenting, she is also well known as a public speaker on children and the media and child welfare. In 1995, Noni Hazlehurst received an Order of Australia for services to children and children's television and in 2007 an Honorary Doctorate of Philosophy from Flinders University (SA).

Dr Renate Klein is a long-term health researcher and has written extensively on reproductive technologies and feminist theory. A biologist and social scientist, she was Associate Professor in Women's Studies at Deakin University in Melbourne until 2006, a founder of FINRRAGE (Feminist International Network of Resistance to Reproductive and Genetic Engineering, www.finrrage.org) and an Advisory Board Member of Hands Off Our Ovaries.

Dr Betty McLellan is a feminist ethicist, author, psychotherapist and committed activist of long standing. One of four women who comprise the Coalition for a Feminist Agenda, and the facilitator of f-agenda, Betty's focus is deliberately local and global. She is the author of *Overcoming Anxiety* (Allen & Unwin, 1992), *Beyond Psychoppression: A Feminist Alternative Therapy* (Spinifex Press, 1995) and *Help! I'm Living With a ~~Man~~ Boy* (Spinifex Press, 1999/2006) now translated into thirteen languages. Her fourth book focuses on the politics of speech as a feminist ethical issue (*Unspeakable: A Feminist Ethic of Speech*, forthcoming).

Professor Louise Newman is Director of the Centre for Developmental Psychiatry and Psychology at Monash University and a child and adolescent psychiatrist working with young children who have experienced abuse and trauma. She is also researching the impacts of early trauma on development. She designs and runs interventions for women who have experienced child abuse and are wanting to be effective parents for their own children.

Dr Lauren Rosewarne is a lecturer in public policy in the School of Social and Political Sciences at the University of Melbourne.

She is also the Associate Director of the Centre for Public Policy. Her first book *Sex in Public: Women, Outdoor Advertising and Public Policy* was published in 2007 (Cambridge Scholar's Press) and her second book *Cheating on the Sisterhood: Infidelity and Feminism* was published in 2009 (Praeger). Lauren has qualifications in political science, cultural studies, public policy and education and has taught and researched in areas including media, feminist studies and American politics.

Dr Emma Rush is the lead author of the reports 'Corporate Paedophilia: Sexualisation of children in Australia' and 'Letting Children Be Children: Stopping the sexualisation of children,' both published by the Australia Institute in 2006. Much of her research work has revolved around ethical issues in public life. She is currently lecturing in ethics at Charles Sturt University.

Melinda Tankard Reist is an Australian author, speaker, commentator and advocate with a special interest in issues affecting women and girls. Melinda is author of *Giving Sorrow Words: Women's Stories of Grief After Abortion* (Duffy & Snellgrove, 2000) and *Defiant Birth: Women Who Resist Medical Eugenics* (Spinifex Press, 2006). Melinda's commentary has been published and broadcast in Australia and overseas. A founder of independent women's think tank Women's Forum Australia, Melinda is editor of the magazine-style research paper *Faking It: The Female Image in Young Women's Magazines* (2007).

INDEX

OTHER BOOKS FROM SPINIFEX PRESS

DEFIANT BIRTH:
WOMEN WHO RESIST MEDICAL EUGENICS
Melinda Tankard Reist

In the face of widespread discrimination against the disabled and a eugenic culture which pathologises disability and crushes diversity, this book radically challenges the status quo.

Defiant Birth tells the personal stories of women who have resisted medical eugenics—women who were told they shouldn't have babies because of perceived disability in themselves or shouldn't have babies because of some imperfection in the child. They have confronted the stigma of disability and in the face of silent disapproval and even open hostility, had their children anyway, in the belief that all life is valuable and that some are not more worthy of it than others.

ISBN 9781876756598

MAKING SEX WORK:
A Failed Experiment with Legalised Prostitution
Mary Lucille Sullivan

Can a prostitute be raped?

Are pregnancy and STIs an Occupational Health and Safety issue?

What sort of society buys and sells women and children for sex?

Does legalisation solve the dangers of sex work?

Sex worker advocates have argued for many years that legalising prostitution is the way to make the industry safer both for workers and clients. In 1984, the State of Victoria did just that, and in this book, Mary Lucille Sullivan looks at the evidence of Victoria's experience, and asks whether the concept of sex work as 'a job like any other' matches the reality. Discussing the practicalities of brothels as regular businesses, the author unearths astounding facts about both the legal and illegal sectors. Covering issues such as violence, organised crime, women's health, and mainstream businesses' involvement in the sex trade, *Making Sex Work* is a compelling read.

> 'Never before has there been such a detailed body of work specifically documenting and challenging the liberal acceptance of the legalised prostitution industry.'
>
> —Carole Moschetti, Journal of Women and Policing

ISBN 9781876756604

NOT FOR SALE:
FEMINISTS RESISTING PROSTITUTION AND PORNOGRAPHY
Christine Stark and Rebecca Whisnant (Eds)

This international anthology brings together research, heart-breaking personal stories from survivors of the sex industry, and theory from over thirty women and men—activists, survivors, academics and journalists. *Not For Sale* is groundbreaking in its breadth, analysis and honesty.

> 'Loving and militant, practical and prophetic, this book collects the least compromised writing on a most crucial problem of our time— even the bottom line issue of all time.'
>
> —CATHARINE A. MACKINNON

ISBN 9781876 756499

THE IDEA OF PROSTITUTION

Sheila Jeffreys

In the *Idea of Prostitution*, Sheila Jeffreys explores the sharply contrasting views of prostitution. She examines the changing concept of prostitution from White Slave Traffic of the nineteenth century to its present status as legal and explodes the distinction between 'forced' and 'free' prostitution, documenting the expanding international traffic in women. She examines the claims of the prostitutes' rights movement and the sex industry, while supporting prostituted women. Jeffreys' argument is threefold: the sex of prostitution is not just sex; the work of prostitution is not ordinary work; and prostitution is a 'choice' not for the prostituted women, but for the men who abuse them.

ISBN 9781875 559657

TRAUMA TRAILS: RECREATING SONG LINES:
THE TRANSGENERATIONAL EFFECTS OF TRAUMA IN INDIGENOUS AUSTRALIA

Judy Atkinson

Providing a startling answer to the questions of how to solve problems of generational trauma, *Trauma Trails* moves beyond the rhetoric of victimhood, and provides inspiration for anyone concerned about Indigenous and non-Indigenous communities today. Beginning with issues of colonial dispossession, Judy Atkinson also sensitively deals with trauma caused by abuse, alcoholism and drug dependency.

Then, through the use of a culturally appropriate research approach called *Dadirri: listening to one another,* Atkinson presents and analyses the stories of a number of Indigenous people. From her analysis of these 'stories of pain, stories of healing,' she is able to point both Indigenous and non-Indigenous readers in the direction of change and healing.

ISBN 9781876756222

*If you would like to know more about Spinifex Press,
write for a free catalogue or visit our website.*

SPINIFEX PRESS
PO Box 212, North Melbourne
Victoria 3051, Australia
women@spinifexpress.com.au
+61 (0)3 9329 6088
www.spinifexpress.com.au

Many Spinifex books are now also available as eBooks.
See the eBookstore on our website for more details.